What a great plan to create a great marriage, even if you're not living in one now. Before you give up hope on the marriage of your dreams, read *Happy Spouse . . . Happy House.* This game plan works.

—Steve Arterburn,
best-selling author of *Every Man's Battle* and *Every Man's Marriage*

Pat and Ruth Williams have created a book on marriage that dispenses encouragement for couples who want to go from good to great, as well as for those marriages that are struggling and need hope. They use clear biblical principles, real-life and engaging examples, and throughout the book, a great positive tone of "you can do this." You will enjoy and learn from this book.

—Dr. John Townsend,
psychologist, leadership consultant, and author
of the two-million best seller *Boundaries*

The timeless wisdom and practical advice in this amazing book will equip you with the tools you need to live a more fulfilled life. *Happy Spouse . . . Happy House* is the culmination of years of experience from two of the greatest parents and spouses you will ever encounter. Pat and Ruth have earned the right to become your parenting and marriage coaches. After raising nineteen children, they have some profound things to say about home life and relationships. If you only read one book this year on marriage and the home, make it this book!

—Jentezen Franklin,
senior pastor of Free Chapel in Gainesville, Georgia,
and *New York Times* best-selling author of *Fasting*

Pat is a great friend of mine whom I respect so very much. This book addresses the core of America's decline—the breakdown of the family because of broken relationships. Without a strong family presence in the lives of our young people—especially in my community, the black community—we will see a further decline in the character of the next generation and future of our country.

—John Perkins,
founder and president of the John M. Perkins Foundation

Pat and Ruth Williams write from the heart in this insightful and helpful marriage manual. My wife Betsy and I feel this book will strengthen couples tremendously, no matter how long they've been married.

—Bobby Richardson,
former New York Yankees second baseman

Pat and Ruth have put together a marvelous book on how to build an exciting and successful marriage. Every couple, and those anticipating marriage, will be greatly blessed from the Scriptures, quotes, and personal experiences that are shared. Highly recommended! I know this book will help your marriage be all that God intended it to be.

—**Dr. Henry Blackaby,**
pastor, speaker, and best-selling author of *Experiencing God*

I am thrilled that Pat and Ruth Williams have shared their many real-life experiences in this important new book. As a result of reading their insights, I am confident that many marriages will be strengthened. The Lord will be honored in the process.

—**Vonette Bright,**
cofounder, Campus Crusade for Christ

Happy spouse, happy house? There is no doubt that this book will help couples learn to put God first, their spouse second . . . and the result will be a happy house!

—**Mark Richt,**
head football coach, University of Georgia

After twenty-one years of marriage, I've learned a truth that Pat and Ruth Williams share in their wonderful book *Happy Spouse . . . Happy House:* "If Mama ain't happy, ain't nobody happy." You will enjoy their encouraging book, whether your marriage is A-OK, a little rocky, or hanging at the bone.

—**Dr. Kevin Leman,**
author of *Sheet Music* and *Turn Up the Heat*

"Happily ever after" is a big fat myth—but this engaging book will point you to the truth. Pat and Ruth Williams show how you can have true happiness in your marriage. Don't miss out on this winning message.

—**Drs. Les and Leslie Parrott,**
founders of RealRelationships.com and authors of *Love Talk*

The Bible has all of the answers. Does it have the answer to America's problems, its moral and economic decline? God answered that over three thousand years ago, and included it in his holy Bible. Now, break this down into units. First man and woman, then home, and then community, city, state, and country. Pat and Ruth pick it up with *Happy Spouse . . . Happy House.* That's where it begins.

—**Bobby Bowden,**
head football coach, Florida State University

Happy Spouse...
Happy House

Happy Spouse...
Happy House

THE *BEST* GAME PLAN FOR A WINNING MARRIAGE

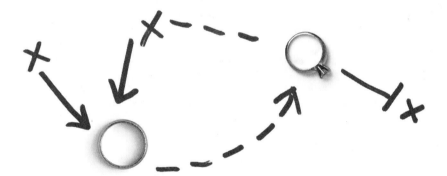

PAT AND RUTH WILLIAMS

WITH DAVE WIMBISH

Standard®
PUBLISHING

Cincinnati, Ohio

Published by Standard Publishing, Cincinnati, Ohio
www.standardpub.com

Editors: Dale Reeves and Lynn Lusby Pratt
Cover design: The DesignWorks Group
Interior design: Andrew Quach

ISBN 978-0-7847-2356-2

Library of Congress Cataloging-in-Publication Data
Williams, Pat, 1940-
  Happy spouse--happy house : the best game plan for a winning marriage / Pat and Ruth E. Williams ;
with Dave Wimbish.
      p. cm.
  Includes bibliographical references.
  ISBN 978-0-7847-2356-2 (perfect bound)
  1. Marriage--Religious aspects--Christianity. I. Williams, Ruth E., 1948- II. Wimbish, David. III.
Title.
  BV835.W547 2009
  248.8'44--dc22
                              2009027649

15 14 13 12 11 10 09   1 2 3 4 5 6 7 8 9

TO BURKE AND DIANE ELLZEY,
RUTH'S BROTHER AND SISTER-IN-LAW,
WHO HAVE LIVED THE PRINCIPLES IN THIS
BOOK FROM DAY ONE OF THEIR MARRIAGE
THIRTY-ONE YEARS AGO.

Contents

Chapter 1

Midnight Phone Call

LET THE WIFE MAKE THE HUSBAND GLAD TO COME HOME,
AND LET HIM MAKE HER SORRY TO SEE HIM LEAVE.

—MARTIN LUTHER

I was just drifting off when the phone rang.

Jarred awake by the shrill sound, I sat bolt upright in bed and began groping in the darkness for the receiver.

The glow from the digital clock told me it was almost midnight.

Who could be calling at this hour?

My heart pounded. Every nerve tingled. As any parent would, I breathed a quick prayer that all my children were safe and well.

I finally grabbed the phone on my fourth try, just as Ruth clicked on her bedside lamp.

"Hello," I croaked.

Silence.

"Hello?"

"Who is it?" Ruth asked.

Finally, a trembling male voice came over the line.

"Is this . . . Pat Williams?"

"Yes it is."

"Of the Orlando Magic?"

"That's right."

I sounded a lot calmer than I was feeling.

"I'm sorry to call you so late, but I didn't know what else to do." My caller paused to catch his breath, and I sensed that he was close to tears.

> I covered the mouthpiece with my hand and whispered, "He says his wife is leaving him."

"Go on," I urged.

"It's my wife. She says she's leaving me." His voice cracked and moved up an octave or two as he continued. "She says she doesn't love me anymore."

Another long pause. Then, "I've read some of your books on marriage, and I've heard you on Dr. Dobson's show."

A mix of emotions shot through me. Relief that my kids were OK. Anger that a stranger was nervy enough to call me at such a late hour. Then finally, sympathy for this hurting man.

"Who is it?" Ruth asked again. "Is everything OK?"

I covered the mouthpiece with my hand and whispered, "He says his wife is leaving him."

"He?" Ruth asked. "He who?"

I shrugged. "I have no idea."

My wife sighed and threw back the covers. "Let me get you some water." She knew this conversation was probably going to last for a while.

Over the past thirty years, I've received hundreds of phone calls from broken people, most of them men, desperately trying to hang on to their marriages. The only difference between those calls and the one I just described is that, thankfully, the vast majority don't come so late at night.

Most of the men who call tell me they had no idea their wives were unhappy. They had no idea there were any problems in their marriages. They didn't see the warning signs coming until their wives suddenly announced they wanted out.

I've heard it again and again: "I was just so busy at work. But I'm trying so hard now. This is the worst thing I've ever been through."

"I know how you feel," I say. "I know you're panic stricken and you want to get the relationship back to what it was. But whatever you do, don't start whining and begging her to stay. Even if she does stay, she'll be doing it out of guilt, or sympathy, and neither is good."

"Then what should I do? I can't bear the thought of her leaving me."

"I understand. I want you to go to her and tell her that you understand she has a right to walk away from the marriage if she wants to, but that you love her and want your marriage to last forever. Tell her, 'If you stay with me, from now on I'm going to do everything I can to be the husband and partner you really want me to be. I know I've failed in many areas, but I'm really going to try to make it work if you'll give me a chance.'"

"Then what?"

"I'm going to lay out a plan for you that will win back your wife's heart—99 percent guaranteed."

If it were possible, I'd be willing to have a telephone conversation with every hurting husband and wife in America. But because that's impossible, I've decided to write this book and share everything I'd say if we were having a nice long chat on the phone. So pull up a chair, settle back, and I'll tell you how you truly can have a happy spouse *and* a happy house.

My wife, Ruth, will be here too, to share from a woman's perspective and to tell you how good I am when it comes to practicing what I preach. Right, Ruth?

We'll both be sharing insights from our own marriage, telling you honestly about some of the challenges we've had to face and how we've overcome them.

Of course, Ruth and I are both aware that thousands of books have been written on the topic of marriage. Go into any bookstore, check out the "Marriage and Family" section, and you'll see what I mean. But I believe the very best of them was written in the early 1980s by Dr. Ed Wheat. His book, *Love Life for Every Married Couple,* literally transformed my life.

Dr. Wheat was a medical doctor in Springdale, Arkansas, who was puzzled that he could not find a medical reason for the health complaints of many of his female patients. The women said they didn't feel good. They were depressed. Sad. Some were certain they were dying of a mysterious disease.

Yet test after test came back clear. Apparently, there was nothing at all wrong with these women.

Or was there?

When the good doctor took a closer look, he discovered that all of them had something in common: an unhappy marriage.

Their bodies weren't broken, but their spirits were.

Test after test came back clear. Apparently, there was nothing at all wrong with these women. Or was there?

This discovery prompted Dr. Wheat to write his wonderful book. In it, he took the position that if even one of the partners in a marriage is committed to the relationship, it can be restored. Dr. Wheat taught that even if your spouse has "fallen out of love with you," you can win her (or him) back by using the principles Ruth and I have built upon in writing this book.

Dr. Wheat's position was that every Christian marriage should be the best the world has ever seen. He even broke his teaching down into the acrostic BEST:

Blessing

Edifying

Sharing

Touching

These four elements are just about fail-proof when it comes to building a solid marriage. They work.

- If your marriage is broken and you want to fix it, this book is for you.
- If your marriage is OK, but not as good as you'd like, Ruth and I will tell you how to rediscover the passion you once knew.
- If you have a strong marriage, we'll suggest how you can make it even better.
- And if you're about to get married, this book will help you learn how to keep your love alive as the years go by.

We're writing to everyone who is married, or contemplating marriage. We know what we're talking about. I speak from experience when I talk about the pain of a marital breakup. I know the trauma of rejection. My first wife left me—with eighteen children.

My oldest children—Jimmy, Bobby, and Karyn—were born during the first six years of my first marriage. My wife frequently talked about adopting children from another country, but I wasn't really interested and hoped her desire would pass. Instead, it grew stronger, to the point where I believed our marriage was at stake.

Thus it was that two- and three-year-old sisters Sarah and Andrea came from South Korea to join our family. I fell in love with them the moment I saw them, and they were a constant delight.

> My marriage slowly wound its way through divorce court and I became a single parent to eighteen children.

A year later, my delight was increased when Michael was born to us.

Next, twins Stephen and Thomas came from South Korea to join the Williams family just prior to their sixth birthdays. And when I heard about four young boys who had been living on the streets in the Philippines, I said, "We've got to help them!" That's when David, Peter, Brian, and Sammy made it an even dozen. After that, Gabriela and Katarina, two beautiful five-year-old orphans from Romania, made it fourteen.

Then, on a trip to Brazil, I met four more desperate kids. Without help, they probably wouldn't make it to adulthood. Well, there was always room for one more—or four more. Welcome to the family, Daniela, Richard, Caroline, and Alan.

A month after their arrival, my wife announced that she wanted out of the marriage. The next three years were awful, as my marriage slowly wound its way through divorce court and I became a single parent to eighteen children. This was a painful, depressing period for me. I was devastated emotionally and financially, and sometimes thought I would never recover.

That's when God surprised me with joy and brought two unexpected treasures into my life.

The first treasure: my wonderful wife Ruth, with whom came the inspiration for sharing the principles that go into building a great marriage.

The second treasure: our nineteenth child—Ruth's lovely daughter, Stephanie.

As legendary broadcaster Paul Harvey would say, "Now you know the rest of the story."

At the end of every chapter, we'll include a list of questions that can be used for personal reflection and further study. If you really want to get the most out of this book, study it together with other couples in a small group setting. During the course of this book, we may touch on some areas that are painful for you. Please keep in mind that our goal is never to cause hurt or open old wounds, but rather to bring healing and hope. We're not here to point fingers, cause hurt feelings, or induce guilt. We've certainly made our share of mistakes. Thank you for reading everything we have to say with a loving, open attitude.

The BEST is yet to come as you read through the pages that follow. I'm so glad you're along for the journey. No matter what the state of your marriage may be—top of the world or bottom of the junk heap—get ready for a transformation.

Reflect & Discuss

1. What do you hope to get out of reading this book?

2. What are the strongest aspects of your marriage?

3. In what specific ways could your relationship with your spouse be improved?

4. Take a few moments to think about how you felt when you were first falling in love with your partner. What made you fall in love with your spouse?

5. Which of your spouse's qualities were (and hopefully still are) most attractive to you?

6. What are the happiest moments you and your spouse have spent together? What made those times so special? Describe how you felt.

Part 1: The Power to Bless

Chapter 2

Bless Your Spouse,
Bless Yourself

ALL OF YOU SHOULD BE OF ONE MIND. SYMPATHIZE WITH EACH OTHER. LOVE EACH OTHER AS BROTHERS AND SISTERS. BE TENDERHEARTED, AND KEEP A HUMBLE ATTITUDE. DON'T REPAY EVIL FOR EVIL. DON'T RETALIATE WITH INSULTS WHEN PEOPLE INSULT YOU. INSTEAD, PAY THEM BACK WITH A BLESS-ING. THAT IS WHAT GOD HAS CALLED YOU TO DO, AND HE WILL BLESS YOU FOR IT.

—1 PETER 3:8, 9

For Kevin, five years of marriage was more than enough. The time had come to pull the plug.

The marriage was on a protracted downhill slide, and picking up speed. Kevin remembered that he had once loved Rita intensely, but wondered how that had ever been possible. He now thought of her as self-centered, inconsiderate, boring, and spiteful. She was also a poor housekeeper and at least fifteen pounds heavier than on their wedding day.

Kevin used his friend Eric as a sounding board. The two played golf together every other Saturday during the spring and summer, and Eric had grown accustomed to his companion's constant complaining. Today was no exception.

Kevin groaned as he hooked yet another ball into the woods.

"Sorry, buddy," Eric sympathized. "Looks like it's not your day."

"I know. I can't keep my mind on my game. It's"—Eric knew what was coming—"Rita. I tell you, I've had it with that woman."

Eric smiled and tried to change the subject. "Come on. Let's see if we can find your ball."

Kevin reached out and touched his pal's arm. "I mean it this time," he said. "I'm going to ask her for a divorce."

"Are you sure?"

"Absolutely." Then half to himself, he said, "She's made my life so miserable. I just wish I could find a way to get even with her for everything she's put me through."

"Are you serious?" Eric asked.

"You know I am."

"Then I have an idea."

"Let's have it," Kevin demanded.

"OK, listen." Eric looked around to make sure no one was eavesdropping. "Treat her like a queen."

> "A divorce? No way! I'm married to a goddess! I can't believe you thought I should leave her."

"Treat her like a queen?" Kevin took a step backwards. "What kind of a dumb idea is that?"

"Hear me out. Start treating her like you think she's the most wonderful woman in the world. Do things for her. Buy her little presents. Tell her how beautiful she is. Take her off for a romantic weekend."

"And then?" Kevin asked.

"Just when you've got her convinced you think the world of her—*bam!*—that's when you walk out the door. She will be devastated!"

Kevin nodded. "I like it!"

Because he had to go out of town on business, Eric missed their next golf date. So it wasn't until a month later that he and his friend were back on the greens.

"So, how's your plan working?" Eric asked, as Kevin bent over to set up his tee for the first hole.

"Plan?" Kevin scratched his head as he stood up straight.

"You know. You told me how you'd had it with Rita. And I suggested—"

"Oh, *that* plan?" Kevin smiled and shook his head. "You know, it's really funny. You wouldn't believe how much Rita has changed over the past few weeks."

"Changed? How?"

"Well, I did what you said. I started treating her like I think she's the most wonderful woman in the world, and now she is!" He threw up his hands in a gesture that said, *Can you believe it?*

"So . . . you don't want a divorce then?"

"A divorce? No way! I'm married to a goddess! I can't believe you thought I should leave her."

It's too bad every dissatisfied husband—and wife—doesn't have a friend as wise or as patient as Eric.

He knew something extremely important: when you treat people as if they are special, they become special. It may be that your attitude toward them changes their behavior. Or it could be that the way you treat them changes your own attitude. More than likely, it's a little bit of both.

The first step in The BEST Game Plan for a Winning Marriage is utilizing the power God has given you to bless, rather than harm, your spouse.

> Anyone who blesses another person will himself be blessed.

You can love her, build her up, encourage her, and bless her. Or you can criticize her, tear her down, discourage her, and in essence, curse her.

As God spoke through the apostle Peter, anyone who blesses another person will himself be blessed. I believe this is doubly true for a man who actively looks for ways to bless his wife, for as the Bible says in the second chapter of Genesis, a married couple is one flesh. It follows, then, that if you treat your wife in a way that makes her feel unfulfilled and unloved, you are also hurting yourself, since you are an extension of your mate.

What Happened to "Happily Ever After"?

Nobody knows for certain how many marriages will end in divorce, but it's a huge number. The organization Americans for Divorce Reform estimates that "probably, 40 or possibly up to 50 percent of marriages will end in divorce if current trends continue. However, that is only a projection and a prediction."[1]

That's terrible!

But I've got worse news. According to the highly respected Barna Research Group, things aren't any better among Christians.[2] As a matter of fact, a Barna survey found that "divorce rates among conservative Christians were significantly higher" than for other groups, including nonbelievers!

Barna says, "While it may be alarming to discover that born-again Christians are more likely than others to experience a divorce, that pattern has been in place for quite some time."

He found that 34 percent of adults who consider themselves to be "nondenominational Christians" are divorced. So are 29 percent of Baptists, 25 percent of "mainline Protestants" and 21 percent of both Lutherans and Catholics. Overall, 27 percent of born-again Christians are divorced, compared with 24 percent of other Christians, and 21 percent of those who have no religious faith at all.

I know I'm throwing a lot of statistics at you. That comes naturally because I've spent most of my life in professional sports, where a player's stats are so important. We measure a player's ability by things like field goal percentage, free throw percentage, batting average, fielding average, yards per carry, and so on.

> The rules for building a happy marriage have been around for thousands of years.

And when I see a statistic that tells me over a fourth of all Christian marriages end in divorce, I know immediately: That stinks!

Some have challenged Barna's findings. They just don't believe that Christian marriages are failing at the same rate as those involving non-Christians. But as far as I know, no one has presented any solid evidence to show that he got it wrong.

How did we ever get so far from the way God planned it to be? After all, the rules for building a happy marriage have been around for thousands of years—as long as the existence of marriage itself. In fact, the one who created marriage (God) outlined his rules for a happy, healthy marriage in his book (the Bible).

You may be a believer who readily accepts everything the Bible has to say on every subject, a nonbeliever who doesn't want to hear anything the Bible has to say, or anywhere between those two places. Whichever describes you, I want to tell you that the principles we'll be talking about in this book will work for everyone. They have been tested and proven true during thousands of years of human history.

> Notice that this passage says the man was expected to stay home and "bring happiness" to his wife, rather than the other way around.

The Bible places a very high priority on the marital relationship between a man and a woman. In the second chapter of the Bible, we read that "a man will leave his father and mother and be united to his wife, and they will become one flesh" (Genesis 2:24, *NIV*). Here's what my hero, the late Dr. Ed Wheat, had to say about the "leave" in this verse: "If it is necessary to leave your father and mother, then certainly all lesser ties must be broken, changed, or left behind. . . . This means that you and your mate need to refocus your lives on each other, rather than looking to another individual or group of people to meet your emotional needs."[3]

Deuteronomy 24:5 says, "A newly married man must not be drafted into the army or be given any other official responsibilities. He must be free to spend one year at home, bringing happiness to the wife he has married." This law was written at a time when the young nation of Israel was fighting for its life. The Israelites were constantly under the threat of attack, and when war came, every able-bodied man was needed. But the law of Moses said that marriage was more important. Notice that this passage says the man was expected to stay home and "bring happiness" to his wife, rather than the other way around.

Are you proactive in trying to make your wife happy? That's what God expects of you.

Bless Your Spouse in Word and Deed

Blessing is a word that is flipped around endlessly, especially in church circles. Somebody sneezes and we say, "Bless you." At a meal someone asks, "Will you ask the blessing?" As we're shaking hands with the pastor on Sunday morning, we say, "Pastor, that sermon was such a blessing."

I'm not saying that we're insincere. It's just that we use the word so many ways, it loses its meaning. More importantly, we tend to think we can bless people by simply saying "Bless you" and not putting any action behind it. Any man who wants to have a great marriage must learn to bless his wife *daily*—encouraging, pleasing, and praising her.

Are You Giving 100 Percent?

Nancy Reagan was once asked in an interview, "Is your marriage a 50-50 proposition?"

She said, "No, it's a 100-100 percent proposition."

Nancy was right. Some people make the mistake of thinking that marriage is a 50-50 proposition.

It's not.

Marriage is a 100-100 deal.

For a marriage to be everything it can and should be, both partners have to be giving it everything they've got. Having spent my life in professional sports, I can tell you that no coach would ever be satisfied with a 90 percent effort from his players. Nothing less than 100 percent will do.

> Having spent my life in professional sports, I can tell you that no coach would ever be satisfied with a 90 percent effort from his players.

Coaches expect their players to "leave it all on the court." This means giving every ounce of energy in pursuit of a victory. How could we give our life partners anything less?

Let's face it. It's human nature to think we're giving 100 percent when we're really giving much less. Therefore, a husband and wife who think they're giving their all may actually be doing just enough to meet each other halfway.

Have you ever heard an athlete say something like this? "We gave 110 percent out there." I've heard it more times than I can count, usually in an interview after a winning effort, and I always think, *No you didn't. That's impossible.* You can't possibly give more than 100 percent. That's the maximum. Giving 110 percent would be like spending $110 when you only had $100. It's just another example of how most people tend to overestimate the effort they're making.

In Matthew 5:41, Jesus said, "If a soldier demands that you carry his gear for a mile, carry it two miles."

For Jesus' contemporaries, this must have been one of the most difficult of all his teachings. In Jesus' day, all of Palestine was under Roman rule. According to the law, if you were not a Roman citizen, any of Caesar's soldiers had the right to stop you at any time and ask you to carry his equipment for one mile.

> If Jesus commanded us to go the extra mile for our enemies, how much more do you suppose he expects us to give ourselves to our spouses?

It didn't matter what you were doing. If a soldier beckoned you, you had to go. If you were working in your field, you dropped your hoe and went off to assist him. If you were on your way home from the market, you put down your bags and went with him. No excuse was accepted. It was even worse than being summoned for jury duty! Anyone who refused to go faced swift, severe punishment—even death.

It's difficult to imagine how much the Jewish people hated the Romans. And yet Jesus said, in effect, "Do what they ask . . . and more. Show them God's love through your compassionate obedience. Return good for evil."

Jesus was also saying, "When you think you've done enough, you've really only gone halfway—so you've got to put twice as much effort into everything you do."

If Jesus commanded us to go the extra mile for our enemies, how much more do you suppose he expects us to give ourselves to our spouses?

Try a Little Kindness

The old song says, "You always hurt the one you love." Tragically, it seems that the old song has hit the bull's-eye.

It is one of life's enduring mysteries that many husbands and wives will say mean things to each other that they wouldn't dream of saying to complete strangers.

The husband complains that the women in the office seem to appreciate him when his wife doesn't. But no wonder. When he's around the women at work, he acts like Prince Charming. When he comes through the door at the end of the day, he suddenly turns into Ivan the Terrible.

The wife gets appreciative comments from the men at work that let her know she's "still got it." But she doesn't even try to look good when it's just her and her husband at home.

This is what happens when a husband and wife have stopped cultivating their marriage and allow their passion to die. Maintaining a healthy marriage is sometimes hard work. But Ruth and I are here to tell you that it can be done.

Several years ago, I attended a dinner honoring Eddie Robinson, the legendary football coach of Grambling University. Robinson, who has since passed away, was eighty years old at the time. He told the gathering that he and his wife had been married for sixty-one years, but still held hands everywhere they went.

"In fact," he said, "we like to walk on the Grambling campus, holding hands, so the young people can see us and realize that marriage can be permanent and couples can stay in love their entire lives."

William Penn said, "Between a man and his wife nothing ought to rule but love."[4] And Tim A. Gardner explains,

> Too many people view marriage as a destination rather than a journey. . . . When the goal is marriage, we know enough to court our mate-to-be in a way that will create a stronger attraction between us. We win the heart of our beloved and get married. Then . . . we move on to the next big goal. But that isn't how God intended marriage to work. Getting married is only one point in time. *Staying* married—in a way that is exciting and fun—is a process. I have a plaque in my office that says, "Getting married is easy; staying married is more difficult; staying happily married for a lifetime should rank among the fine arts."[5]

A few years ago, the National Survey of Families and Households asked 5,232 American adults to describe the state of their marriages.[6] Some 645 of these people described themselves as "un-happily married." Five years later, the same organization tracked down all those people to see what had happened to them and their marriages. Not surprisingly, many were divorced, although a considerable number had worked through their problems and were still with their first husband or wife.

> Those who had walked away from their unhappy marriages were no happier than those who had hung in there and worked things out.

And here's the big surprise: Those who had walked away from their unhappy marriages were no happier than those who had hung in there and worked things out. In fact, Waite and her colleagues found that "divorce did not typically reduce symptoms of depression, raise self-esteem, or increase a sense of mastery." What about those who had decided to stick in there? Two-thirds who had once described themselves as "unhappily married" now said their marriages were happy. More remarkable, almost 80 percent of those who had described their marriages as "very unhappy" now called themselves happily married.

The moral of the story is obvious: don't give up on your marriage. Work at it, and you can make it better.

I can guarantee you that your marriage will go through some stormy seas. Every marriage does. But that's no reason to bail out. If your marriage boat has sprung a leak, get busy and fix it.

Writer Simon Presland says, "Some people view conflict and confrontation as a win-lose situation. These spouses see being right as far more important than the marital relationship. But working out a hurtful issue is not about who's right and who's wrong. Your goal should not be to win, but to confront a conflict and restore the harmony in your relationship."[7]

Great advice. Any man who thinks that winning an argument is more important than his relationship with his wife is a fool. Jesus asked, "What do you benefit if you gain the whole world but lose your own soul?" (Matthew 16:26). In the same way, what will it benefit you if you win argument after argument, but lose your marriage in the process?

RUTH SAYS

In *The 7 Habits of Highly Effective People,* habit 4 is "Think win-win."[8] It's the first habit of relationships, and there are basically four common paradigms of human interaction: lose-lose, lose-win, win-lose, and win-win. If I am a win-lose person, I always want my way. For many people the attitude is "It's my way or the highway." The win-lose person only looks out for himself and doesn't care who he hurts along the way. If I am a lose-win person, I let people walk all over me. I always give in because I do not want to argue; I just want peace at any price, and therefore, I will not stand up even when I'm right. In either case, whether I'm a win-lose person or a lose-win person, the relationships in my life will always end up lose-lose—especially the marriage relationship.

> If I think win-win in every interaction, I am looking out not only for me but also for the other person.

In a marriage, no one can win all the time and no one should lose all the time. If that happens, the marriage will not be a happy one, no matter how many years it lasts. If I think win-win in every interaction, I am looking out not only for me but also for the other person. And if I'm looking out for the other person, we are much more likely to end up in harmony. It's all about having an abundance mentality, about wanting the best for my spouse, about sharing with my spouse. It's not about being selfish or insisting on getting my way all the time.

One of the things that has made our marriage so successful is that we are both looking out for the other in every situation. We want each other to be successful. We want to be a blessing to each other, not a hindrance. We want to make life easier for each other.

Here's some brilliant advice from poet Ogden Nash:

> To keep your marriage brimming,
> With love in the loving cup,
> Whenever you're wrong, admit it;
> Whenever you're right, shut up.[9]

The apostle Paul said it a little bit differently: "Husbands ought to love their wives as they love their own bodies. For a man who loves his wife actually shows love for himself" (Ephesians 5:28).

He couldn't have said it better. Bless your wife and you bless yourself.

Reflect  & Discuss

1. List at least five specific ways you can bless your spouse during the next twenty-four hours.

2. What are the five things you appreciate most about your spouse?

3. What does your spouse like you to do for him or her that you should do more often?

4. In what ways has your husband or wife blessed you during the past week? Be as specific as possible.

5. What kind of blessing would you like to receive from your spouse more often? Does he or she know how you feel?

6. Take another look at 1 Peter 3:8, 9. In which areas do you feel you do a good job of living up to Peter's words?

7. Where do you fall short? What steps can you take to improve in these areas?

8. First Corinthians 16:14 says, "Do everything with love." How can you apply this verse to your daily interactions with your spouse?

9. Name at least one specific area of your life together where you will begin making a sincere effort to do everything with love.

Top Ten Ways to Bless Your Spouse

MARRIAGE IS NOT A NOUN; IT'S A VERB. IT ISN'T SOMETHING YOU GET. IT'S SOMETHING YOU DO. IT'S THE WAY YOU LOVE YOUR PARTNER EVERY DAY.

—BARBARA DE ANGELIS

I spend a lot of time in hotel rooms. If I'm not on the road with the Orlando Magic, I may be giving a motivational talk to the executives of a Fortune 500 company, appearing on a TV or radio sports talk program, or running in a marathon somewhere around the country.

Somewhere in the Midwest not too long ago, I came into my room late at night and clicked the television on to see if I could get the latest news. As the screen flickered to life, an old black-and-white sitcom from the '60s came into view. I started to change the channel, but then realized it was a classic episode of *The Dick Van Dyke Show*, "The Night the Roof Fell In."[1]

After more than forty-five years, this episode still stands out as a very funny, and yet painful, example of what can happen in a marriage when both partners are focused on themselves rather than each other. It all starts when the show's two main characters, Rob and Laura Petrie, both have a bad day—Laura at home and Rob at the office.

As soon as Rob walks through the door, it's clear that disaster is on the way.

Neither wants to listen to what the other has been through. Instead of sympathizing with each other and finding comfort in their relationship, each seems determined to outdo the other in a childish game of "my day was worse than yours." Their argument quickly escalates out of control, and Rob storms out of the house, saying that he doesn't know when he'll be back.

The scene shifts to the next day, when we see Rob and Laura telling their friends about their argument. Neither version has much to do with the truth.

In Laura's version, she has prepared a lovely candlelit dinner and is wearing one of her most beautiful gowns when her husband walks through the door. When she goes to kiss him, he shouts at her, "Don't kiss me! I have a cold sore!" Next he glares at her and says, "Why don't you fix yourself up?"

He then asks, in a disgusted tone, "What is that smell?"

When Laura replies that she's fixed one of his favorite dinners, he snarls, "Open a window."

He's angry that their son hasn't said anything cute today. "What's the use of having a kid if he never says anything cute?" He kicks the furniture. What a jerk!

But then there's *his* side of the story. In his version, he dances through the door like Fred Astaire, only to be greeted by an angry wife in a baggy sweatshirt, demanding to know where he's been. His reply, "Counting the hours until I could be with you," doesn't seem to change her sour mood. When he tries to tell her that he's sorry she's had such a bad day, she interprets it as meaning that he's sorry he married her, and orders him out of the house.

It's all hilarious—and a little painful too. That's because just about every married couple has been there at one time or another. Of course, because this is a 1960s sitcom, everything is neatly resolved within thirty minutes, and we know that Rob and Laura Petrie will quickly put this sorry episode behind them and go on to live happily ever after.

Unfortunately, such incidents aren't always so easy to overcome. Harsh words leave sore spots that can flare up again at the smallest provocation. Such selfish behavior can cause long-term damage to a marriage. So what can we do? After all, human beings are selfish creatures by nature. Self-preservation is the natural inclination of any man or woman.

Apparently, it's been that way since we first appeared as a species. Take a look at Genesis 3:12 and see how Adam reacted when God asked why he had sinned. He didn't skip a beat: "It's the woman's fault." I wonder how Eve felt when her husband tried to pin the blame on her. She probably thought, *I can't believe it. Is this the same man who said he loved me so much he'd be willing to do anything for me—even give his life for me?*

> "For husbands, this means love your wives, just as Christ loved the church."

Husbands need to learn to love their wives in accordance with Ephesians 5:25, 26: "For husbands, this means love your wives, just as Christ loved the church. He gave up his life for her to make her holy and clean, washed by the cleansing of God's word." Paul wasn't talking about marriage when he wrote these words to the church at Philippi, but they certainly apply: "Make me truly happy by agreeing wholeheartedly with each other, loving one another, and working together with one mind and purpose. Don't be selfish; don't try to impress others. Be humble, thinking of others as better than yourselves" (Philippians 2:2, 3).

Do your actions demonstrate to your wife how much you love her? Are you willing to sacrifice in order that she can be blessed (encouraged, pleased, and praised)? No matter how good you may think you are when it comes to blessing your wife (and thus, your marriage), there are ten ways to do even better.

1. Bless Your Spouse by Speaking Well of Her

Proverbs 18:22 says, "The man who finds a wife finds a treasure, and he receives favor from the LORD." Does your wife know that you value her and consider her to be a treasure from God? Do other people know you love your wife and thank God for her?

How do you talk about her to your friends when she's not around to hear? Do you call her "the old ball and chain," or use similar derogatory language because you don't want your friends to think you're a romantic wimp? The words we speak impact us more than we know. I believe that if we act as if we love someone, we will come to love her. I also think the reverse is true. If we act as if we don't care about someone, as if she is a bother and a nuisance, we will come to see her as a bother and a nuisance.

Don't put your wife down. Ever! Speak well of her at all times.

I don't watch a whole lot of television because I don't have the time. But one program that catches my eye from time to time is *Antiques Roadshow* on PBS. I love it when someone brings in an old chest or vase or another item that he's been keeping in a back room somewhere and finds out that it's worth several thousand dollars. It's wonderful to see the look that comes across someone's face when he realizes that he's owned something extremely valuable, but he's been letting it collect dust in an out-of-the-way corner.

Do you suppose he'll put that ten-thousand dollar painting back on a shelf in the closet when he gets home? Of course not! That masterpiece is going to be displayed in a prominent place where everyone can see it.

I believe that millions of men and women could have, *would* have wonderful joy-filled marriages if only they knew how incredibly valuable their spouses are. If you treat your marriage as if it doesn't really have any value, you'll drain all the life and love right out of it.

In my professional life, my number one goal is for the Orlando Magic to win the championship of the National Basketball Association. When that happens, you'd better believe I'm going to celebrate like crazy. I won't go around moaning, "Oh, we won that stupid championship. Now everyone will expect us to do it again. It's just more pressure on top of pressure." Everyone I come into contact with will know how thrilled I am.

> If you treat your marriage as if it doesn't really have any value, you'll drain all the life and love right out of it.

Well, you know what? A good marriage is worth more than an NBA championship. Do yourself and your spouse a favor and let everyone know how grateful you are for the person you married.

I speak fifty to sixty times a year to corporate groups, civic organizations, and educational institutions about subjects such as leadership, teamwork, and self-motivation. One of the things I consciously work into whatever I'm speaking about is a bragging moment about my wife, Ruth. I met her when she spoke one year at our Magic executive retreat. I thought she was *very* impressive—so much so that I married her a couple of years later. But I digress.

Ruth is a senior consultant and speaker for the FranklinCovey organization. You may use the FranklinCovey planner as a tool to manage your time, and you're probably familiar with her boss's (Stephen R. Covey) best-selling book, *The 7 Habits of Highly Effective People*. Ruth is a fantastic teacher in her workshops. I know. I've watched her, and others tell me after they've heard her speak.

One of the ways I bless her is by speaking highly of her in my own speeches. For example, I always challenge people in my audience to keep learning. It's what keeps us on top of our game. And one of the things I mention is that my wife, Ruth, is currently working on her PhD in organizational leadership. "In a couple of years, she'll have it . . . and I'll be married to Dr. Ruth." That always gets a laugh, but it also lets people know how proud I am of my wife.

> It would be hard *not* to value her when I am constantly bragging about her to thousands of people each year.

So even though she is not there to hear it, others hear it, and, more importantly, I'm speaking it. It would be hard *not* to value her when I am constantly bragging about her to thousands of people each year.

RUTH SAYS

What Pat says is true. Because he speaks to so many different groups across the country, many of the people who come to my seminars have heard him speak. It never fails. Whenever someone makes the connection between Pat and me, they say things like: "Now I know where I've heard about you. I heard your husband speak at our national convention last year and he was GREAT! ("Thank you," I say. "And yes, he is wonderful.") And man, does he love you! He gave you a really good plug in his speech. I can't wait to hear what you have to say today!"

I'm sure that if someone had a camera and took my picture

at that moment, he would see a huge grin on my face and a sparkle in my eye as I'm thinking, *Thanks, honey.* What a wonderful way to start my workday. What a lift for my spirits! My day can't help but go great with a beginning like that.

It stays with me all day and I can't wait to get home and give Pat a huge hug for making me look so good. And, guys, it doesn't take much—just a few short sentences built into a two-hour speech, but those few words said about me when I'm not even there make me very grateful that I am married to Pat.

And . . . he gets more hugs at the end of the day.

2. Bless Your Spouse with Acts of Kindness

Believe it or not, living in Florida has a few drawbacks. These include sand spurs, palmetto bugs the size of small tanks, and a wee bit of humidity from time to time. But these are far outweighed by the warm weather in the winter, the beautiful beaches, and of course, the fruit. Everything grows in Florida, including every conceivable variety of citrus.

I learned a long time ago that one of Ruth's favorite ways to start the day is with a juicy pink grapefruit, sliced up just right, so that the wedges slide easily into her spoon. It's not hard for me to help her start the day that way. It takes a couple of minutes to walk outside and find the best-looking grapefruit on the tree. Then perhaps another five minutes to slice it up and set it on her vanity. We're talking ten minutes tops. But it means so much to Ruth.

She knows it's a unique way for me to say "I love you."

- It shows that I pay attention to her and have learned what she likes.
- It reinforces the thought that I want to take care of her, which is something I believe every woman wants (even those who aren't willing to admit it).

When I take the time to fix Ruth that grapefruit first thing in the morning, I can do no wrong the rest of the day.

And it gets even better for me if I help her end her day on a high note—which for Ruth means a relaxing, hot bath. If she doesn't get her bath, her day's not complete. (Needless to say, she's not the type of gal who wants to spend her vacation camping in the Sierras.) My job is to run the bathwater. I take great pride in making sure it's just the right temperature and depth for her to slide in and wash away the stress of the day. If you're old enough, you may remember the Boston Celtics' Red Auerbach and his famous cigars. Whenever Coach Auerbach lit up one of his cigars near the end of a game, everyone knew the victory was in the bag. When the bathwater starts running in the Williams house, that means the day is coming to a victorious ending.

Ask yourself what little loving acts you did for your spouse in the early days of your marriage. How about before you were married, when she was your girlfriend? Do you still do those little things for her? If so, good for you. If not, why not?

Just as I was preparing to sit down to write this book, the New York Yankees invited me to come to Tampa and take part in one of their winter Fantasy Camps at George Steinbrenner Field. Although most people think of me as being connected to professional basketball, I grew up playing baseball and still love the game. I played college ball at Wake Forest, and then spent a couple of years as a catcher in the Philadelphia Phillies organization. It's always fun to get back out on the diamond—even if crouching down behind home plate is a bit harder on the knees than it used to be.

Just in case you don't know what I'm talking about when I say Fantasy Camp, let me explain. All the Major League Baseball teams run winter camps where guys who love the game, but never got to play professionally, put on a uniform and practice with former big-league players for three or four days. Then, on the last day, the ex-major leaguers square off against the campers in a series of games.

As I was in the dugout just prior to the start of the first game, I struck up a conversation with former Yankee Homer Bush. Homer is a good guy who had a solid six-year career in the majors. I asked what he was up to these days, and he told me that he was living in Dallas and enjoying life with his wife, Monica, and their children.

Then he smiled and said, "Monica said something to me the other day that really made an impression on me. She said, 'Whatever you did to get me, you'd better keep doing it if you want to keep me!'"

I nodded, "Boy, that's good advice for any husband."

Do you remember what you did to get your wife to fall in love with you? Did you stop doing those things almost as soon as she said "I do"? If so, take a tip from Monica Bush.

> She said, "Whatever you did to get me, you'd better keep doing it if you want to keep me!"

You can't possibly go wrong by showing your wife, through your actions, that you love her. And here's a wonderful concept I picked up from a friend of mine, a best-selling author and speaker by the name of Hal Urban: bless your wife by treating her as if she were a guest in your house. In other words, show her the same kindness and courtesy you would show someone you care about who had come a long distance to spend a few days with you.

Urban was a guest on my radio show once, and we got to discussing 1 Corinthians 16:14, where the apostle Paul tells us to "do everything with love." Urban told me that he had just been out on the road for four days, and he decided to do his best to live up to Paul's words. He said, "Everywhere I went, I practiced doing everything with love. Everyone I met—cab drivers, hotel clerks, waiters, cashiers—I treated with respect, courtesy, patience, and love."

He admitted that it wasn't easy. Not everyone is naturally lovable. Still, Urban said, "When I got home, I told my wife I'd just had the four best days of my life."

I was just heading out for a short trip myself, so I decided to follow Hal's example, and you know what? I too had a wonderful time. I discovered that when you smile at someone, you'll generally get a smile back. When you treat people with respect and patience, they'll treat you the same way. Of course, there are exceptions. Some people won't be nice to you no matter what you do. But if you make up your mind in advance that you won't let those folks get to you, that you'll just keep on loving them no matter what, you're going to save yourself a lot of unnecessary aggravation. And I've discovered a tremendous freedom in the realization that I don't have to let other people control my attitude or behavior. If the other guy wants to act like a jerk, that's his business. I don't have to get down on his level.

If you can get a good reaction from people you don't even know simply by treating them as if you care about them, just imagine the good reaction you will get from your spouse.

RUTH SAYS

In *The 7 Habits of Highly Effective People*, habit 1 is: Be proactive.[2] One of the things that indicates whether you are proactive or reactive is your choice of actions to take. That's right, I said your choice. We all choose how we respond to any stimulus or situation. Some choose to respond positively, while some choose to respond negatively—but it is a choice.

> In so many cases, one or both partners have developed the habit of negative behavior toward the other.

Pat shared the platform with Naomi Judd at a Peter Lowe Success Seminar years ago, and she said something that has stayed with me ever since. She said, "We have choices and we make them. Nobody's doing it to you; you're doing it to yourself. You're only a victim once; then you're a volunteer."

In a marriage, we all have the choice to show kindness to our spouses or not to. However, in so many cases, one or both partners have developed the habit of negative behavior toward the other. In *The 7 Habits* book, Stephen shares the story of a man who confides in him at the end of a seminar. The man says, "Stephen, I like what you're saying. But every situation is so different. Look at my marriage. I'm really worried. My wife and I just don't have the same feelings for each other we used to have. I guess I just don't love her anymore and she doesn't love me. . . . And we have three children we're really concerned about. What do you suggest?"

"Love her," Stephen replied.

"I told you, the feeling just isn't there anymore."

"Love her."

"You don't understand. The feeling of love just isn't there."

"Then love her. If the feeling isn't there, that's a good reason to love her."

"But how do you love when you don't love?"

"My friend, love is a verb. Love—the feeling—is a fruit of love, the verb. So love her. Serve her. Sacrifice. Listen to her. Empathize. Appreciate. Affirm her. Are you willing to do that?"[3]

When I share this story in the workshop, I get all kinds of questioning looks. Many people don't believe this can be done. But remember Kevin and Rita from chapter 2 of this book? When Kevin made love a verb and began doing things that made Rita feel like a queen, he became the king. And those feelings from their dating years returned.

So—it can happen if you are willing to do it. Give it a try.

3. Bless Your Spouse with Thanks and Affirmation

I couldn't possibly list all of the things Ruth takes care of during an "ordinary" week. But here's a sampling:

- She looks after the needs of all nineteen children with their growing number of husbands and wives, plus seven grandchildren. (Can you imagine keeping track of all those birthdays?)
- She has a full-time career.
- She handles all the mail that comes into the house.
- She keeps the pantry and refrigerator stocked.

- She finds time to work on her PhD.
- She makes the bed—every day.
- She makes sure the house is neat and inviting. (People who see it for the first time think a decorator did it. Ruth is the decorator—and she does it at bargain prices.)
- And—oh yes—she handles all the finances and pays the bills. (I'm not good at it and she is.)

I could go on for pages. If you take the time to think about what your wife does for you and your family, you'll probably see that she does a lot more than you ever realized. If you don't already do so, please take the very next opportunity to tell her how much you appreciate everything she does.

Don't assume she knows how much you appreciate her. Unless you tell her, she doesn't know.

RUTH SAYS

Pat's assistant, Latria Leak, married Chris Leak in February of 2008. Yes, I am referring to *the* Chris Leak, the quarterback who brought the University of Florida to a national championship in 2006, just in case you were wondering. However, Chris has become a championship husband as well. Recently Latria received flowers from Chris at the office—for no special occasion. Just because. Here's the card he attached:

> To my wife, the love of my life and my best friend. Thank you for all that you have done for me. You have changed my life in ways I couldn't imagine and I appreciate all the little things, as well as the big sacrifices you have made for me. Thank you for showing me the way to our Lord and Savior, Jesus Christ, and the foundation he

has laid for us. You are my idol, my hero, and I just want you to know I love you more and more every day. I'm the luckiest man in the world to have you by my side. Thank you, honey. I love you.

Here is a young man who understands how to bless his wife, and I would predict that they are in for a long and happy marriage.

According to Dr. Shruti S. Poulsen, a continuing lecturer at Purdue University's Department of Child Development and Family Studies, in order for a marriage to thrive, there must be five positive interactions between a husband and wife for every negative reaction.[4] She writes: "Stable and happy couples share more positive feelings and actions than negative ones. . . . Partners who criticize each other, provide constant negative feedback, aren't supportive of each other, don't demonstrate affection or appreciation, or behave uninterested in their partner are in relationships that are out of balance." She goes on to say, "Let your partner know what you appreciate. Thank him or her for what he or she does for you. Compliment your partner. Point out the positives that you genuinely appreciate."

> In order for a marriage to thrive, there must be five positive interactions between a husband and wife for every negative reaction.

Dr. Poulsen has some good suggestions for improving the number of positive exchanges between a husband and wife. I've adapted them here:

- Start by keeping a journal for one week.
- At the end of each day, sit down and review the interactions you've had with your mate during the past twenty-four hours. On one side of the page, list the interactions that you would categorize as positive. On the other side of the page, list the negatives.

- At the end of every week, review your journal to see how you're doing. Are there five times more positives than negatives? If not, you need to work on improving communication with your spouse.
- Decide that you will implement two positive actions from your list on a regular basis.
- After a few weeks of this, keep another journal to see if your positive-to-negative ratio has improved. If not, look for more ways you can be proactively positive in your relationship with your spouse.

My own feeling is that five positives for every negative is a good rule of thumb. But a marriage between believers ought to be a lot better than that. We ought to give at least ten positives for every negative—and even then, we could learn to do better.

Be honest with yourself. Have you slipped into the habit of criticizing your wife? Do you complain when she cooks something you're not crazy about, let her know she needs to lose a little weight, or criticize the way she disciplines the children? If you do, make up your mind right now that you will stop it.

The next time you find yourself starting to make a critical comment, stop yourself and turn it into a positive. Far too many husbands (and wives) have fallen into the habit of criticizing their mates. The time for change has come.

Here's another way of looking at it. The head baseball coach at the University of Hawaii, Mike Trapasso, sent me his four keys to being a successful coach. One of the keys applies to marriage as well as coaching: choose to be a fountain . . . not a drain.

What does this mean? A fountain is a giver; it bubbles up and supplies a drink of cool, refreshing water. It's a major positive in a marriage relationship. Being a fountain means looking for the positive first, rather than the negative. It means treating your spouse with respect and hoping he or she may actually choose to reciprocate. It's an attitude of giving to your spouse.

A drain, on the other hand, is the opposite. It takes. It sucks the good right out of us and can suck the love and commitment out of a marriage.

Will you choose to be a fountain or a drain in your marriage? The choice you make can either bring more energy and intimacy to your marriage or help to destroy it.

One night in Orlando, I had the privilege of sharing the dais at a dinner with Bill McCartney, former head football coach at the University of Colorado and founder of Promise Keepers.

A few years ago, Promise Keepers events were filling stadiums with men pledging themselves to live honorably with their wives and families and before God. After McCartney retired, Promise Keepers lost a little bit of its fire—so he has now come back to pump some renewed energy into the organization.

Looking out over the room packed with men, McCartney said, "If you want to know the condition of your wife, look at her face. Everything you've invested in her over the years will be seen in that face. Do you see joy, contentment, and splendor? Or hurt, frustration, and emptiness? It's up to you."

A total hush fell over the room as we all let that sink in. We can choose to bless our wives through what we do, or we can tear them down.

RUTH SAYS

I have to brag on Pat for a moment. If I kept a journal each day on the interactions between Pat and me, the positive side would far outweigh the negative side. I could go months without being able to write down one negative thing at all. In fact, I don't even remember the last negative interaction, because he is always making positive deposits.

One of the things I constantly hear wives complain about is that their husbands don't notice what they do around the house.

The interaction goes about like this: The wife has added something new to the house, thinking it enhances the warmth and beauty of the home, and she can't wait for her husband to get home and notice. The husband walks in at the end of the day and he doesn't notice.

The wife says, "Honey, do you notice something different?"

"Did you get your hair done?"

"No." She still has the look of anticipation.

"Is that a new outfit?"

"No." She sighs, but is still hopeful.

"Are you wearing a different perfume?"

"No." She's thinking, *No! You idiot! Are you blind?* but she remains calm.

"Look around," she says. "Notice anything different about the house?" She's got her hopes up again.

"Um . . ." he says, as he is looking around, eyes darting from one corner of the room to the other. He's thinking, *I'm dead. Please, God, I need a revelation and I need it NOW!*

"I'm sorry, sweetheart, but the house looks great—as usual," he says, hoping he can come out of this alive. He really doesn't see anything different, but he doesn't want a depressed, pouting wife for the rest of the evening.

"Never mind," she says, heaving a huge sigh of disappointment. "I put up new window treatments today. Thought it would give the room a lift."

"WOW! You were right. The room does look better. But you know I never pay attention to that stuff."

"I know. I was just hoping . . . I got 'em on sale and installed them myself," she says with downcast eyes. "It's no big deal."

This is a common story that I hear all the time. And these are common statements that go with the stories:

- "He doesn't appreciate what I do in the house."
- "He never notices anything."
- "I don't know why I work so hard keeping the house looking nice; he doesn't really care."

These are hard for me to identify with because Pat notices just about everything. I do bargain shop, and I love Stein Mart for home accessories. One day I decided I needed (well, wanted) a table by a chair near one of the windows of our TV room that looks out on the lake. It couldn't be bulky, as that would block too much of the view.

About a week later, I found the perfect table at Stein Mart. It was gold metal and lightweight with a glass top, so it wouldn't obstruct the view. Another plus was that it would give me a place to put some books and pictures, and if someone was sitting in the chair next to it, a drink could be placed on it.

> And every now and then, he says, out of the blue, "Thank you for making our home so beautiful and comfortable."

Pat had been out of town for several days, and I had truly forgotten about the addition of the table. After all, I had been looking at it for days. I was watching a movie in the TV room, waiting for him to get home, when I heard his car pull into the driveway.

The first thing Pat does when he gets home, whether it's at the end of a single day or a week, is hug and kiss me. He walked into the TV room and did just that. Then he said, looking over my shoulder as he hugged me, "Hey, I like the new table by the window. It really makes that corner come alive." I beamed inside and gave him an even bigger hug and kiss.

"Thanks for noticing."

I love it when he notices things I've done around the house. He has made it a habit to really look around when he comes home, and I appreciate that. And every now and then, he says, out of the blue, "Thank you for making our home so beautiful and comfortable." That sends me over the happy edge!

4. Bless Your Spouse Through Prayer

I have not listed these first four ways to bless your spouse in order of their importance. Every one is absolutely vital to the health of the marital relationship. Asking which is most important would be like trying to choose between air, water, or food. You can't do it, because all are essential.

But if I'd had to list in order of importance, I would have put prayer first. Praying for and with your wife is so important. I believe that one of the primary reasons why so many marriages fail—even Christian marriages—is that the husband and wife don't take the time to pray for and with each other.

In their book *Couples Who Pray*, Squire Rushnell and Louise DuArt highlight the benefits of praying together. Squire noted that research shows a 20 to 30 percent increase in romance, conversation, and overall happiness when couples commit to five minutes of prayer together for forty days. They've launched an emphasis to encourage couples to take their forty-day prayer challenge and reap the joys of being prayer partners with one another.[5]

Praying with each other brings a couple closer together. There is just something about seeking God together that creates a deeper heart connection between a man and woman who already love each other. There is a supernatural strengthening of the marital bond.

There is a tendency for Christian couples to get so busy that they don't take the time to pray with each other—and believe me, Ruth and I both know what that's like. With two full-time careers and nineteen children in the mix, we've spent many days in such a frenzy of activity that we literally

> There is just something about seeking God together that creates a deeper heart connection between a man and woman who already love each other.

fell exhausted into bed at night. But we eventually came to see that if we were too busy to pray with each other, we were just *too* busy. If your schedule is so full that it doesn't allow time for prayer, change your schedule.

Here's another reason why praying for your spouse is so important: it allows you to see into the depths of her heart. Do you know what her deepest concerns are? Are you aware of her greatest hopes and fears? What does she need from the Lord? If you haven't already done so, ask your wife how she would like you to pray for her; then follow through. If there is a particular issue she wants you to pray about, ask her what is going on in that area of her life.

Suppose she tells you that she's hit a rough spot with one of her friends, and feels a bit hurt and rejected. Then not only pray about that situation, but ask her about it. It will mean more to her than you can possibly know when you say, "Hon, I've been praying about that situation between you and Sue. Have things improved?"

She will be delighted that you listened, that you care, and that you have made her concerns your concerns. No matter how good your marriage might be right now, praying for your wife will certainly make it better.

In his book *The Making of a Man*, Richard Exley asked his male readers a few important questions like: What is your wife's greatest concern? greatest need? wildest dream? And he indicated that guys who don't know those answers don't know their wives as well as they think they do.[6] How can a man love his wife as he should if he doesn't know her very well?

> "I believe that if every Christian couple would pray together regularly, our nation would experience a spiritual renewal of historical proportions."

Ouch!

Any man who prays for his wife as God expects him to will most certainly know the answer to all (or at least most) of those questions.

Dennis Rainey, president of the Christian organization FamilyLife, says, "Surveys at our FamilyLife Marriage Conferences indicate that less than 8 percent of all couples pray together on a regular basis. . . . I believe that if every Christian couple would pray together regularly, our nation would experience a spiritual renewal of historical proportions, including a dramatic drop in the Christian community's divorce rate." He adds, "I urge you to make this commitment with your spouse. You may be afraid to start, and let me assure you, you are not alone. Many people are hesitant to start praying with their spouses. If this is the case, try saying this prayer: 'Lord, teach me how to pray with my spouse. I'm afraid.' I can promise you; [praying with your spouse] will be one of the most rewarding things you will ever do for your marriage and your family."[7]

Every man should pray for God's highest blessing on his wife. This is a powerful request that God loves to answer. Frankly, some men are afraid to pray this way because they are threatened by their mate's success. I believe that the Bible clearly teaches that the man is to be the spiritual head of his family (Ephesians 5:22-24). I believe that men are to protect, care for, and provide for their wives. But I also believe that one of the most important things we can do is to provide our wives with the security and freedom to bloom, thrive, and fulfill every ounce of potential God has placed within them.

Just because God chose me, as the man, to be the head of my house, doesn't mean that I am superior to Ruth in any way. It doesn't mean that I'm supposed to control her, keep her down, or expect her to live out her life in my shadow. I'm proud that Ruth is a shining star for her company. I'm delighted that she is an eloquent public speaker. I'm thrilled when people tell me that I was lucky to get such a beautiful and intelligent woman to marry me, because I know they're right! I'm not even jealous when I read something she's written and realize that she's even a better writer than I am. (Well, not too jealous anyway.)

It's exciting for me to see God blessing Ruth in so many ways, and her success has contributed to the strength of our marriage. The same can happen to you.

RUTH SAYS

Praying together and having a husband who is the spiritual leader of the home makes all the difference in the world. Notice I said *leader*, not dictator. There is a major difference.

Another sad story I hear from women is how controlling their husbands are. People often come up to me after workshops, asking for advice. Sometimes they e-mail or call me after a seminar, wondering if I can help them. (Pat's not the only one who gets phone calls.) I have a master's degree in psychology and have done some counseling in the past, so it's easy for me to slip into that role.

There are two issues that are very difficult to work through in a marriage: a controlling spouse and a spouse of a different faith or no faith at all. In fact, I would tell single women, if you see either of these in a person you're dating, run—run now, and run far—and never look back. Get away! You're far better off being single than ending up with someone who tries to control you or who tries to pull you away from your faith.

> There are two issues that are very difficult to work through in a marriage: a controlling spouse and a spouse of a different faith or no faith at all.

A young woman named Kristen approached me and said, "I need help. How do I deal with a controlling husband?"

My answer: "Don't let him." But that's easier said than done many times. So just for the record, let me say this about the issue of control. If a man (or woman) needs to control you, it's because he is insecure in some way. Controlling you is the only way he can feel good about himself.

Kristen said, "I know he's smarter than me, and he works and makes all the money. I just stay home with the baby."

"Whoa! *Just* stay home with the baby? Dr. Laura would give you a gold medal. Is that what *you* want to do?"

"Yes, I love taking care of my house and the baby, but Dan is always telling me that since he makes all the money, he should control what we do with it. I get an allowance, but he even goes to the grocery store with me—not because he likes buying groceries, but because he doesn't want me to spend money on things he doesn't like. Sometimes I can't even get things for the baby that I want to try."

So much for a partnership. Marriage is a partnership in every sense of the word, not just in living arrangements. So everything should be discussed between partners—especially money. As I questioned her further, I discovered that Dan was not a spiritual person. He had been raised in a particular faith but did not practice it. And prayer was nonexistent in that family.

She wanted to go to church and pray together, but he always blew it off. So Kristen, like so many other young women, will have to hack her way to church every Sunday alone with the baby, probably with an argument before leaving the house about how "our whole day will be ruined" or "by the time you get home, the day will be just about over." I've heard them all—from men who don't want to go to church, but they don't want their wives and children to go either. It's so sad.

A relationship with a truly spiritual man is the Super Bowl of marriage. Before the kids all left home, we had a ritual every morning at the breakfast table. Everyone would get their food and Pat would have devotions. They complained, of course, as kids do, but it's something that every one of them remembers with a smile today.

One of our rituals each night at bedtime is for Pat to read the Bible to me with some kind of devotion, story, or discussion. What a way to end a day! It wipes away all the dust of the day, and problems I've encountered during my day seem so much smaller. I so miss it when he's out of town. It's very special.

> Kristen, like so many other young women, will have to hack her way to church every Sunday alone with the baby, probably with an argument before leaving the house.

After being married to Pat, I know what the word *cherished* means, and one of the reasons is his spiritual attitude toward everything. There's a loving kindness that is beyond sweet.

Yet he's so very masculine. But because he's comfortable with himself and is grounded in Jesus, his attitude toward others, especially me, is different. It's meek, yet bold; kind, yet strong; considerate, yet self-assured. I've told my daughters not to settle for anything less. They'll be cheating themselves and their children if they do.

5. Bless Your Spouse with Words of Love

Don't think, *She knows I love her*. She needs to hear it. Often. Three little words. So easy to say. And yet so powerful. Why don't we say them more often? I've never heard anyone say with regret, "I'm just sorry that I told her so often that I loved her." I *have* heard people say, "I wish I had told her more often that I love her." How long has it been since you told your spouse that you love her? Do you tell her every day? How long has it been since you've sent her a love note?

> I've never heard anyone say with regret, "I'm just sorry that I told her so often that I loved her." I *have* heard people say, "I wish I had told her more often that I love her."

Here's a great idea: Take a few minutes to stop into the nearest greeting card store and buy several "I love you" cards. Then, every so often, mail one of them to her. It will mean more than you can imagine when she finds that card from you as she's going through the mail (and we all know mail is mostly bills) at the end of the day. You can also leave cards or love notes around the house where she'll find them—on her dresser, on the kitchen table, on your bed.

Someone says, "Pat, if I did that, my wife would think for sure I was feeling guilty about something." If you haven't done it for a while, she might, at first. But it's the kind of thing a woman can get used to. (But not so used to it that it won't thrill her.) When you bless your wife this way, you're going to find out that you are blessed too. Jesus said, "Give, and you will receive. Your gift will return to you in full—pressed down, shaken together to make room for more, running over, and poured into your lap. The amount you give will determine the amount you get back" (Luke 6:38).

Experience has shown me that this verse is especially true in the marital relationship. When you give love, you get love in return. Plus, you get the wonderful warm, fuzzy feeling that comes from knowing you are making your wife happy and treating her the way God wants you to. (Yes, I know that there are exceptions to every rule. There are some people who are so far from God that they insist on returning evil for good and hatred for love. For example, I would never counsel a woman to keep showing self-sacrificing love to a man who is physically abusive. My advice would be to pray for him—from a safe distance.)

RUTH SAYS

People often ask, "When did you know you were in love with Pat?" At the very beginning. We met the day I spoke to the Magic executive team. At the end of the seminar, Pat came up to me and introduced himself and asked if he could help carry my equipment to my car. He also said he wanted to give me a book he had just written.

As he was signing *Go for the Magic*, we began talking. Two hours later, I was on my way to the airport to go to Dallas. He departed for New Orleans. We both had speaking engagements the next day. We traded business cards and said our good-byes. That evening he called and left a message, and I returned the call. From that day on, we've talked to each other every evening—by phone if we're in different cities.

It doesn't matter what time it is or how many hours difference there are. He always times it so that I get a call before 11:00 PM my time. Sometimes it's a one-minute call; sometimes much longer, but that call always ends with "I love you."

He feels good. I feel good. I get flowers. He gets a big kiss. *Happy couple!*

Let me tell you, it's hard *not* to have a good marriage when you hear those words every single day.

And I'm not sure just how he does it, but when I leave town and open my suitcase at my destination, there is *always* a card or a simple note telling me how much he misses me (even if it's just for one night) and that he loves me.

Sometimes when he goes out to run in the morning, he comes back with fresh-picked flowers. He'll put them in a coffee cup or glass and bring them to me with a big smile on his face. It's another way of saying "I love you." He feels good. I feel good. I get flowers. He gets a big kiss. *Happy couple!*

6. Bless Your Spouse with Compliments

Tell her she's beautiful. If you think she looks especially nice today, tell her so. If you liked that meal she prepared, let her know. The more specific you are in your compliments, the more they will be appreciated. Let her know that you notice her and appreciate who she is and what she does. Does she know you think she's a good cook? What else do you appreciate about her? Her sense of humor? Her intelligence? Her tender heart? Her organizational skills? I believe that you should never pass up an opportunity to compliment someone—especially if that someone is your spouse.

Gene Conley is one of the few people who was so talented he made it to the big leagues in two sports. Gene was so good he spent eleven years as a Major League pitcher and seven seasons in the NBA. He played for a World Series championship, three NBA championships, and was the winning pitcher in the 1955 Major League All-Star game. When you ask a guy like that for his favorite memory, you can bet that he's got plenty to choose from.

I had the privilege of having lunch with Gene a couple of years ago, and he told me that he will never forget something that happened to him in 1959:

"I had just joined the Phillies. We were playing the Cardinals in a double-header. I was down in the bullpen when manager Eddie Sawyer called and said, 'Get Conley ready.'

"It was the bottom of the ninth, two on, two out, and Stan Musial [one of the greatest hitters in the history of the game] at the plate."

Conley struck out Musial to end the game.

"As I walked off the field, Sawyer was standing by himself on the dugout steps. He reached out his hand and said, 'Thanks, Gene. I appreciate what you did.'"

Gene is a big, strong, rugged man, standing six feet eight, who always intimidated hitters due to his imposing presence on the mound. But his eyes clouded up as he related that story. "That happened nearly fifty years ago," Gene said, "and I still get emotional when I think about it."

> "I never criticize my players until they're convinced of my unconditional confidence in their abilities."

Those few words from his manager gave Gene Conley a blessing that lasted a lifetime. At the other end of the spectrum, a few careless, cutting words can create a wound that never heals.

John Robinson, former football coach of the Los Angeles Rams and the University of Southern California, once told me, "I never criticize my players until they're convinced of my unconditional confidence in their abilities." Good words. No wonder he had so much success on the football field. And a long-lasting marriage to boot. He and his wife, Linda, raised six children together.

RUTH SAYS

Perhaps you've seen this commercial for a low-fat cereal. The wife is sitting at the breakfast table, eating a bowl full, when the husband walks up and asks, "So, honey, you trying to watch your weight?"

"Do I look like I need to watch my weight?" she retorts with a raised eyebrow.

"No, honey, it's just that the box says it's low in fat," he says sheepishly, and further tries to backpedal.

Then she asks sarcastically, "So—what else does the box say?"

"The box says, 'Shut up, Steve,'" he replies.

I laughed the first time I saw that commercial, because his first comment was so innocent, yet not very well thought out. It was so typical and so typically taken the wrong way. I am constantly amazed as I watch couples who are married (supposedly happily) cut each other to shreds. Sometimes it's in front of the spouses; sometimes behind their backs. Sometimes it's a small thing; sometimes big. And it makes me so thankful that Pat does just the opposite.

I don't care if we are going out for breakfast in our sweats on a Saturday morning or to a gala ball, Pat always has a compliment about how I look. It may be, "Wow! You look good in black today!" Or, "Your hair is different. I like it." Or a whistle and, "Man, I'm glad you're with me tonight." He's always giving me compliments and I return them with compliments of my own, like, "How's my hunk today?"

Whether he's complimenting me on what I've done in the house or something I've accomplished, my spirits are lifted for the rest of the day. And it doesn't take much—one sentence spoken genuinely and heartfelt. It's more icing on the cake and life is much sweeter.

PS: A note to the ladies. If you want compliments, make sure you give him something to compliment you about. It's hard to compliment someone who always looks like death warmed over. Now, don't get mad. We'll cover this more in the chapter on touching.

7. Bless Your Spouse by Really Listening to Her

Don't roll your eyes, or stare off into space like you're not really interested. It won't cost you anything to pay attention. But it will do wonders for your marriage. And when I say listen, I mean just that. Don't feel that you have to tell your wife what to do or solve her problems. More than anything else, she needs you to listen to her. If your wife asks you to listen and you start giving advice, you have not done what she asked. If she is pouring out her heart to you and you start giving her ten reasons why she shouldn't feel the way she does, or tell her she's overreacting, you are belittling her. If she asks you what you think she should do about a particular situation, tell her, certainly. But otherwise, you can show her how much you love her simply by listening.

> If your wife asks you to listen and you start giving advice, you have not done what she asked.

Although I don't have any hard facts to back it up, I've heard the following and I believe that it's generally true. When a man and woman first begin dating, they enjoy learning everything they can about each other. But once they get married, it doesn't take long for the learning to stop. Theoretically, if you had a newly in-love couple, took the man and the woman into separate rooms and asked them questions about their partner, they'd be able to correctly answer almost everything. But if you took a couple that had been married fifteen years or so and did the same, you'd probably be surprised by how little they knew about each other.

Are you saying, "It's not that way in my marriage"? I hope so. But let's take a little quiz and find out whether you really listen.

1. What is your spouse's favorite color?
2. Where was your spouse born?
3. What is your spouse's mother's maiden name?
4. Can you name your spouse's all-time favorite movie?
5. What about her all-time favorite book?
6. What is your spouse's favorite food?
7. Does your spouse have a favorite song? If so, what is it?

8. What is your spouse's favorite Bible verse?
9. What kind of pets did she have when she was a child?
10. Does she have a favorite perfume?

How many of these did you know? If you got at least seven of them right, give yourself a pat on the back. You've done a fairly decent job of keeping your ears open. However, missing any of these simple questions is an indication that you have much to learn about your spouse. After all, these questions merely scratched the surface of who she is. There is so much more to know down in the depths of her soul.

RUTH SAYS

Habit 5 in *The 7 Habits of Highly Effective People* is "Seek first to understand, then to be understood."[8] In the participant guidebook, there is a quote, an old Native American proverb, on the introduction page to Habit 5 that says, "Listen, or your tongue will make you deaf."

When I ask groups, "So what does that mean?" the answer is simple. It means shut up and listen. And this is more than just hearing. It's truly understanding the other person so well that you can almost put yourself in his or her shoes. It's empathic listening. That's the kind of listening Pat is talking about—really listening to get it.

If you search online, you'll pull up a wide variation in numbers, but there is a consensus that women speak far more words per day than men do. (You knew that already.) So, men, you have a lot more to listen to. But here's the kicker: sometimes it's just the listening that is needed.

Men seem to be born with a fix-it gene. They want to solve problems right away, tackle them, and move on to the next one.

Women, on the other hand, often just want someone to listen to what they're saying—without solving it necessarily—just listen. That "just listening" is a true gesture of love and caring.

In my workshop, I share a story (that I got from a devotional book) about this very subject. A minister (could be an engineer, accountant, or salesman) comes home from work one day and asks his wife, "So, honey, how was your day?"

> Men seem to be born with a fix-it gene. They want to solve problems right away, tackle them, and move on to the next one. Women, on the other hand, often just want someone to listen to what they're saying— without solving it necessarily.

She immediately begins to tell him about the kid's earache, the flat tire she had on I-4, the repairman she had to call about the washing machine, and so on.

He immediately begins to tell her what to do about all those things, but she stops him midstream and says, "I've already done all that. I didn't need you to solve them. I just needed you to listen to me."

It's that simple.

8. Bless Your Spouse by Helping Out Around the House

Most wives would be delighted if their husbands would be willing to do little things like setting the table, vacuuming the living room carpet, or some laundry once in a while. For bonus points, you could get down on your knees and scrub the toilets. (If you're going to do the laundry, just make sure you know what you're doing. She's not going to be happy with you if you shrink a couple of her favorite blouses by washing or drying them at the wrong temperature. Take it from a guy who knows.) There are literally dozens of ways you can bless your wife by helping out around the house. It may take you five minutes to set the table for dinner. But a lifetime of marital bliss can be built out of such simple, but thoughtful gestures.

RUTH SAYS

Pat doesn't do laundry; he doesn't do dishes; he is not a handyman; he doesn't do the yard. He's just not a help-around-the-house kind of husband.

In Dr. Gray's Venus and Mars book, he says that many men have some Venus tendencies and many women have some Mars tendencies. That's Pat and me. He is very loving and nurturing and loves to talk—about everything. I always want the bottom line.

We have come to understand this about each other. There are times when he gets into one of his stories and I'm thinking, *What's the bottom line here?* But I don't say anything. I let him talk because he likes to. And there are times when he gets going and sees that I'm not really that into it and he says, "OK, here's the bottom line." Then we both have a laugh about it.

It's kind of the same way around the house. He can't fix things or put toys together, but I can—and when I can't, I call for help.

But there are things he does that help me tremendously. When we first got married, he was one of those "drop it where you take it off" people. He would not make the bed for months if he could get away with it. We talked about these small things (which can later become really big arguments), and he realized that my day would go much better if the bed was made and clothes were in hampers rather than on the floor.

I make the bed every morning I'm at home. I also know that when I'm out of town, the bed does not get made. I also know, however, that on the day of my return, the bed will be made when I walk into our bedroom.

He knows that means a lot to me and he does it—for me.

He also puts clothes in hampers. (Guys, it's not that difficult to do, and it will make your wife's day better—which will make *your* day better.)

Making the bed and putting dirty clothes in the hamper may seem like little things. And yet they mean a lot because I know he does them for me.

Pat is a "read-aholic." He reads five to seven books a week. There are books everywhere in the house. He has books on his nightstand, books waiting to be read in the office, and books that he's already finished in the library. He even talks to his books as he is "putting them out to pasture" in the library.

> He also puts clothes in hampers. (Guys, it's not that difficult to do, and it will make your wife's day better—which will make *your* day better.)

One day he said he wished he could rearrange the library and put books in sections, the way it's done at a public library. That was a major undertaking, but it meant a lot to him, so we began removing eight thousand-plus books (remember, he loves to read) from the shelves and arranging them by topic. I even gave up some of my knickknack space for his books. Why? Because he loves it.

If he can make the bed for me, I can certainly give him shelf space for his books.

If you truly love and care for your partner, it's easy to do meaningful things for him. In a really good marriage, both partners work at making life easier for the other—and the rewards are great.

9. Bless Your Spouse by Courting Her

An acquaintance of mine recently told me that her niece was unhappy in her marriage: "Her husband doesn't believe that people have to go out on dates after they're married." Apparently, this husband thought dating was what you did when you were getting to know someone and deciding whether you wanted to spend your life with her. He saw no reason for dinners, movies, dancing, or any other such activity once the marriage vows had been recited.

I hope you don't believe that. But do your actions show that you don't believe it? Every woman needs to be courted!

> When we're home at the same time, we're often running in different directions trying to stay on track.

Ruth and I do our best to have a date night every week and a date weekend every other month. We both believe this time together is essential to the health and well-being of our marriage.

We are both on the road a lot of the time. When we're home at the same time, we're often running in different directions trying to stay on track. You've heard of ships passing in the night. Often, Ruth and I are running so fast we're like bullet trains passing in the night. *(What was that blur? Oh, that must have been Ruth.)* I don't think we're much different from most families, especially during tough economic times when it can take two incomes to keep a family treading water.

No matter how busy you are, you and your spouse must take some time for romancing each other, for getting away from the daily pressures that come from being a parent, and for just having some fun. And by the way, don't take the kids along. Family vacations are great, but that's not what I'm talking about.

Another important way you can court (and bless) your spouse is by bringing her gifts for no reason at all, except that you love her.

Flowers. A CD of her favorite music. A book. Some earrings. A gift card to one of her favorite stores. It doesn't have to be expensive, but it should be thoughtful. Here's a great opportunity for you to show your spouse that you know enough about her to understand what she likes. It wouldn't be a very good idea to buy her a big box of chocolates when she's on a diet, or a bottle of perfume that she's allergic to or can't stand. Keep your eyes and ears open for clues as to what she might like. Then go out and buy it for her. You probably did this sort of thing to win her in the first place. No reason to stop now.

My wife, Ruth, is a strong, independent, professional businesswoman. But she is absolutely delighted when I do something special to let her know how important she is to me. She loves it when I bring her flowers; or when she's going out of town on a business trip, I sneak a card or note into her suitcase to let her know that I love her and will miss her while she's gone.

RUTH SAYS

This is a biggie, guys. Dating is a must, no matter how long you've been married or what your economic status is. You don't even have to spend money. You can take a walk. You can watch a movie (or ball game, ladies) together at home. You can go to a park and people-watch and talk. What's important here is the time alone together.

When the kids were all at home and much younger and we were going on a date, we would often hear, "A date? You're married. You don't need to date." Like the young man Pat just mentioned, kids think you only date when you're "young." But we tried to teach them that it was necessary for married couples (no matter how old) to date. I think they got it.

We now have seven grandchildren (number eight is on the way) so we get plenty of requests for babysitting. We love to do it, of course. But often, we'll have to turn down the opportunity: "Sorry, can't tonight. Dad and I have a date." Every now and then we hear the sigh on the other end of the phone or see the raised eyebrow when the request is made in person. Then we'll hear, "I know. Married couples need to date. Have fun!"

> Dating is a must, no matter how long you've been married or what your economic status is. You don't even have to spend money.

Hopefully, they really do get it and they'll follow our example. Dating is a critical part of marriage.

10. Bless Your Spouse by Showing Affection

Here's a familiar complaint of married women: "My husband never touches me unless he wants sex."

We'll talk about the importance of touch in part 4. But I do want to say that one of the best ways you can encourage and bless your wife is to show her physical affection. I know, I know. You're a guy, and it doesn't take much touching to get your motor running. But your spouse needs to know that you love touching her, even when it's not going to lead to the bedroom. So hold her hand. Rub her neck and shoulders when she's feeling tired and stressed. Give her plenty of hugs. Ask her if she'd like you to rub her back. Reach over and give her a love pat on the arm. If you're sitting on the sofa watching TV together, put your arm around her.

> I'm talking about two people who share the same living space, who eat at the same table, sit on the same couch to watch television, sleep in the same bed, and yet never touch each other except for sex.

A physical distance between a husband and wife can lead to an emotional distance as well. I'm not talking about a situation where one of you has to be away from the other for an extended period of time. I'm talking about two people who share the same living space, who eat at the same table, sit on the same couch to watch television, sleep in the same bed, and yet never touch each other except for sex—and perhaps even then, not in a loving, kind, gentle way. When you don't bless your wife by demonstrating regular physical affection, you are sending her a message that you don't find her attractive, have fallen out of love with her, or perhaps that you're angry about something.

Ruth and I do our best to "touch" each other, even when we're hundreds of miles apart. (OK, the absolute truth is that she's better at it than I am.) Every morning, when I check the voice mails at my office, I find a message from Ruth. It usually goes something like this: "Good morning, my darlin' (not darling; she's from the South). I know this is going to be a great day for you, doing the things you love. I hope you have a ball. Just wanted you to know that I'll be thinking of you. Can't wait to talk to you tonight. Please get home safely. I'll be so excited to see you. I love you, my darlin'."

You may be thinking, *Oh, please. Too mushy for me.* But I can't tell you what a comfort it is to get a message like that when I'm away from home and longing for the comfort of my own bed. Or when I'm facing a long, tough day, and just don't feel that I'm up to it. Over the last twelve years, there have been only three or four times when Ruth did not leave me a morning message. That was because her day got off to a frenzied start and she just didn't have time to do it. Every time, she's left a message before noon. Experts will tell you that it's essential to eat a good breakfast in the morning, but those short messages are worth far more to me than any breakfast could possibly be.

I also leave messages on Ruth's voice mail, although I'm not going to tell you what I say. That's between my wife and me.

RUTH SAYS

Those phone messages are something we started when we were first dating—and I must admit, they've gotten more poignant and even racier the longer we've been married. Pat is right. Hearing that message every morning is a blessing. It's a definite upper to start the day. Many times that message will stay with me all day long. What a great way to show affection in a nonphysical way!

But physical is good too. Sometimes it's a kiss and hug when Pat walks through the door at the end of the day (and by the way, kids love seeing that; they beam); sometimes it's holding my hand in church; sometimes it's simply laying his hand on my knee as we're driving somewhere. Other times it's a bear hug in the kitchen, or a blown kiss across the driveway. Those affectionate signs say "I love you" and they mean so much.

And, ladies, if you're doing the same kind of things for your man, it stays with him all day. He'll be much less likely to look elsewhere if he's getting all the affection he needs from you.

You may be thinking, *I can't believe it. You two have been married twelve years and you act like a couple of kids.* Exactly. I recommend it for every couple.

You say you're just not the touchy-feely kind? You can learn. Besides, whether you know it or not, you need nonsexual physical affection as well.

> I believe a spiritual blessing is imparted each time we touch someone else in a loving, caring way.

On several occasions in the past, I had the privilege of sharing the podium with Dr. Ed Wheat. What a shock it was to hear the brilliant teaching of this venerable southern doctor, while he was dressed in his T-shirt that read, "I'd rather be snuggling."

Dr. Wheat taught that loving contact between a husband and wife was essential to the well-being of a marriage—especially in bed. I remember him telling me that he had three rules about bedtime snuggling:

1. Go to bed at the same time. (In other words, don't let your wife go to bed while you're staying up to watch the late game on TV.)
2. Get up at the same time. It's important to share that morning cup of coffee together.
3. Get rid of the pajamas and nightgowns. The good doctor felt they got in the way of proper snuggling.

The Bible is full of examples where "the laying on of hands" was practiced. It was used for imparting the Holy Spirit (Acts 8:17, 18), for commissioning for spiritual service (Acts 6:6; 13:3), for healing (Mark 5:23; Luke 4:40), and for giving a blessing (Matthew 19:15; Mark 10:16). Although the Bible doesn't say so, I believe a spiritual blessing is imparted each time we touch someone else in a loving, caring way.

You have the power to bless—and *be* blessed in return. Please don't miss out on the blessing.

Reflect & Discuss

1. What do you value most about your spouse?

2. Proverbs 18:22 says that "the man who finds a wife finds a treasure." List some of the good things your wife or husband has brought into your life.

3. What does your spouse value most about you? (Don't assume you know. Ask!)

4. When was the last time you let your spouse have the last word in an argument? What did that feel like?

5. Most humans have a strong urge to be "right." How can we overcome this urge?

6. How often do you and your spouse pray together? Should you do this more frequently? Read 1 Thessalonians 5:17. In what specific ways can you put this verse into practice in your marriage?

7. When was the last time you bought your spouse a gift "for no reason at all"? What response did you get?

8. Read Ephesians 5:21-25. What does it mean to you to love your spouse as Christ loved the church?

9. In what tangible ways will you commit to show this love in your daily relationship?

Part 2: Edify Your Spouse

Use Words and Actions to Build a Better Marriage

A WORD APTLY SPOKEN IS LIKE APPLES OF GOLD IN SETTINGS OF SILVER.

—PROVERBS 25:11, NIV

Let's begin with a pop quiz. Below are quotes from five famous women.[1] Your job is to match each quote with the woman who said it. Ready?

A. "I don't like my voice. I don't like the way I look. I don't like the way I move. I don't like the way I act. I mean, period. So you know, I don't like myself."

B. "I have days when I just feel I look like a dog."

C. "I understand what it feels like not to like aspects of yourself. There have been times that I have felt really terrible about the way I look."

D. "I'm a giraffe. I even walk like a giraffe with a long neck and legs. It's a pretty dumb animal, mind you."

E. "I had ordered long legs, but they never arrived. My eyes are weird too, one is gray and the other is green. I have a crooked smile and my nose looks like a ski slope."

Now here are the women. Who said what?

1. Michelle Pfeiffer
2. Jane Seymour
3. Sophia Loren
4. Elizabeth Taylor
5. Gwyneth Paltrow

After you've guessed . . . The answers are: A-4, B-1, C-5, D-3, E-2.

Are you surprised that a renowned beauty like Elizabeth Taylor would be so hard on herself? Or that Michelle Pfeiffer would think she looks like a dog? Or by any of the other quotes attributed to these acclaimed ladies?

This just goes to show you that women are their own harshest critics. Even the most talented, lovely woman is likely to get down on herself if she doesn't receive regular reinforcement from the man she loves.

If you want to have the BEST marriage you can possibly have, you must edify your spouse. Here's how you do it:

Encourage

Delight

Involve

Fulfill

Yield

We'll be breaking down E-D-I-F-Y in the four chapters in part 2. Let's dig in.

Encourage

Even though I believe it is primarily the husband's job to encourage and build up his wife, I'm also convinced it cuts both ways. I read about one despondent husband who pointed out what he saw as an obvious disparity in marriage. He asked his pastor, "Why is it that *happy wife* rhymes with *happy life*, but nothing seems to rhyme with *happy husband*?"

Dr. James Dobson of Focus on the Family shared the following:

> I have seen men who entered marriage being secure and confident, but their wives put them down and destroyed their belief in themselves. If a marital relationship becomes competitive and critical, a man's self-

esteem sometimes disintegrates within a short period of time. Men are very vulnerable to women in this way. . . . Most of the books (including my own) tell men that their wives need them to build their self-esteem. That is true, but I believe that the male ego is also very vulnerable. If a woman believes in her man, it makes an incredible difference in how he sees himself.[2]

A friend of mine mentions the same thing in his prayer each morning: "Lord, help me to be a constructive presence in every situation that confronts me today. Help me seek to build up and not to tear down. Help me to be an encourager and not a discourager."

I love that prayer. It says a lot about the way we should interact with others as we go through life—especially with our mates.

The importance of encouragement came home to me one day a few years ago when I was having lunch with my sister Ruth. (That's right—Ruth. Two of the most important women in my life share that name with the great heroine from the Old Testament.) At the time of our conversation, Ruth was in her mid-fifties. She has always been attractive, so I was surprised when she said, "When I was growing up, I don't remember anyone ever telling me I looked nice. Mother, Dad, Carol [my other sister], my dates when I got dressed up for them. I never heard, 'You look terrific!' So I grew up thinking I never looked nice at all."

I thought about it for a moment, hoping I could come up with a few memories that would prove her wrong, but I couldn't. I don't know why none of us ever told Ruth

> "The male ego is also very vulnerable. If a woman believes in her man, it makes an incredible difference in how he sees himself."

how nice she looked. I suppose we just thought she didn't need to hear it because she already knew. But she didn't know, and it caused a hurt she carried well into her adult life.

"Finally," she said, "when I got married, Floyd told me I looked nice. But I don't remember ever being told that by anyone else."

The lesson I learned from this is that I will never pass up an opportunity to offer a compliment or give a word of encouragement. Simple words can matter more than we know.

Think about how the world would be different if everyone acted constructively. No more mean-spirited criticism of others. No more backbiting or gossip. No more making ourselves feel good at someone else's expense. No more put-downs or insults followed by the lame excuse that "I was just trying to be funny." Proverbs 20:3 tells us, "It is to a man's honor to avoid strife, but every fool is quick to quarrel" (*NIV*).

Guys, your wife was not made for teasing, so don't do it. This is one of the primary differences between males and females.

When I was a kid, I fell in love with baseball. Some of my favorite childhood memories involve my dad taking me to Phillies games at old Shibe Park in Philadelphia. I had dreams of playing there someday myself. As it turned out, I never made it to the majors. After playing college ball at Wake Forest, I spent two years in the minors before deciding that my future was not on the field, but in the business end of sports.

> It's fine for a group of guys on a bowling team to make up rude nicknames for each other, such as Ape-Brain, No-Neck, and Pinhead. But women would think that was juvenile and rude (and of course, they'd be right).

Nevertheless, I still love the game, and I'm thrilled when teams like the Phillies and Yankees ask me to come over and catch some of their Dream Week games in Florida. It's amazing to walk into one of those locker rooms and hear former players picking on each other and cutting each other down to size. Some of these guys have been out of baseball for years, but they pick right up where they left off, nipping and carving at each other for all they're worth. They have not mellowed with age.

Sometimes it gets pretty vicious, although it always brings gales of laughter from everyone involved.

Men like to tease each other. We put each other down. We insult each other. We make up rude names for each other. I don't know why, really. It's not like we think Don Rickles is a great role model. Whatever the reason, teasing seems to be an integral part of male bonding. And while that sort of behavior may be OK in the locker room, it is totally out of place in the living room.

Women don't treat each other that way, and they don't expect to be treated that way. It's fine for a group of guys on a bowling team to make up rude nicknames for each other, such as Ape-Brain, No-Neck, and Pinhead. But women would think that was juvenile and rude (and of course, they'd be right). If their names are Lori, Kathy, Jan, and Donna, they'll call each other Lori, Kathy, Jan, and Donna. Am I saying that women don't have a sense of humor? Of course not. It's just that the female sense of humor in general is much more refined than the male sense of humor. I have never met a woman who thought The Three Stooges were brilliant comedians. Most men, on the other hand, find them hilarious.

Good-natured, lighthearted banter is fine. Teasing that has a sarcastic or cutting edge to it is not. The problem with the former is that it can quickly get out of hand and become the latter. Always be gentle and kind, and remember that your wife needs to know that you value and respect her. You must not treat your wife as if she's one of the guys. She most definitely is not.

You probably know men who are mean-spirited and hurtful. They use words that are harsh or belittling, then try to excuse their behavior: "I don't know what she got so mad for. I was just making a joke." The best thing about someone like that is that he serves as a wonderful example of what *not* to do. Anyone who enjoys cutting other people down needs to pray about his or her attitude.

The CEO Didn't Laugh

Whenever I give a speech, I like to start off with a few jokes. And wherever possible, I also like to give them a local flavor.

When I arrived in one town to give a speech before a company, I asked the people who picked me up at the airport if they could think of anything I should reference in my speech.

"Well," they said, "our CEO is really overweight."

"Overweight?" I asked. "And he has a sense of humor about it?"

"Oh yes. It wouldn't bother him at all if you teased him about being fat."

As I would come to find out, not exactly.

In my speech that night, I used every fat joke I know—and the audience loved them. Except for one guy, that is. The CEO.

He called me on the phone as soon as I got back to my hotel. "Mr. Williams, I can't even begin to tell you how much you hurt me tonight. This was one of the worst nights of my life."

Of course, I told him again and again how sorry I was for what I had done. But it was too late. There was nothing I could do to take it back.

I learned a very painful and powerful lesson that night. The book of James hits the mark when it says: "The tongue is a small thing that makes grand speeches. But a tiny spark can set a great forest on fire. And the tongue is a flame of fire. It is a whole world of wickedness, corrupting your entire body. It can set your whole life on fire, for it is set on fire by hell itself" (James 3:5, 6).

Pay Attention to Your Wife

Too many husbands rarely compliment their wives. They don't notice the new hairdo or new dress (except perhaps to complain about the cost).

Two women I know, close friends who are about the same age and size, told me about a rather devious experiment they carried out to see how much attention their husbands were paying to them. The two couples went out for dinner together, and during the middle of the evening, the wives excused themselves to visit the ladies' room. (That's another difference between men and women, by the way. Women always go to the restroom in pairs or groups. Men don't consider this a group activity.) When they got there, they switched outfits.

What do you suppose happened when they got back to their table?

You're right. Absolutely nothing. Neither husband raised an eyebrow. Nobody said anything. Later on, I'm sure each husband wondered why his wife was in such a grumpy mood.

Paying attention to your spouse shows that you care, and it's a tremendous encouragement to her. If your wife has to hint around with you, and lead you by the nose to show you something she's done around the house, it takes all the joy out. She shouldn't have to get you involved in a game of Twenty Questions:

"Do you notice anything new?"

"Um . . . is it vegetable, animal, or mineral?"

"Neither."

"Does it have anything to do with your hair?"

"No."

I can't overstress how important it is to keep your eyes open and pay attention. Do you notice when she gets her hair cut? Do you compliment her on that new dress? When she's spent the entire day scrubbing and cleaning, do you notice how great the house looks? Do you thank her for the time and hard work that went into the preparation of a delicious dinner?

If your wife makes herself beautiful for you or does other things for you, but you fail to notice, she may think, *Why should I bother?* If a husband never notices, a wife may reach the point where she never tries. And who could blame her?

Truett Cathy, founder of the Chick-fil-A restaurant chain, is quoted as saying, "How do you identify someone who needs encouragement? Answer: That person is breathing."[3] How true!

Here are ten encouraging ways to pay attention to your wife:

1. Pray for and with her every day.
2. Show her you love her in ways that she will appreciate. (That may mean sending love notes, helping her out by making the bed, or whatever would mean the most to her.)
3. Keep physically fit. (Do you expect your spouse to stay in shape for you? Then do the same for her.)
4. Ask her what jobs need to be done around the house; then do them. (The ones you can do, that is. Don't take on a plumbing problem if you will make it *worse*.)
5. Do the little things, like opening the car door for her, helping to clear the dishes after dinner, and—dare I say it?—remembering to put the seat down.
6. Involve her in your financial planning. (Many widows find themselves in financial limbo because "my husband always took care of the finances." Don't let this happen to the woman you love.)

7. Share a hobby with her—something the two of you can do together.
8. Anticipate your family's needs and plan ahead to meet them.
9. Honor her by being interested in her personal growth and success.
10. Be gentle and loving at all times.

RUTH SAYS

Pat does all of the above ten things. So guess what? He needs the same. Dr. Dobson is right. Men need encouragement from their wives just as much as wives need encouragement from their husbands. And this is more than just compliments that we talked about in blessing your spouse. It's also about encouraging them to do things they love and complimenting them on their successes.

I hear complaints from women about their husbands' involvement in extracurricular activities such as fishing, hunting, golf, tennis, and team sports. The list is endless. Granted, some men (and women) overdo them and rob their families of their time. I'm not talking about that. I'm talking about men who do take care of their families and then can't even play basketball with the guys without a World War III attack when they get home. Don't do that, ladies.

> It's also about encouraging them to do things they love and complimenting them on their successes.

Pat has been an NBA executive for forty years now. But his first love is baseball. His collection of books on baseball is the biggest in the library by far. One of the things he enjoys most in life is playing in the Fantasy Camp games for the Phillies and the Yankees. I can encourage him to do this—or I can complain about it. So if you were the spouse, which would you rather hear:

"Have a great time, sweetheart, and hit a home run for me! Love you!" or "Do you really have to go? I'll be all by myself and it *is* the weekend. (Then the lips go into pout mode.) Come on. Stay home, please!"

"Honey, you know I can't do that. I've already made the commitment. I can't let them down at this point."

"OK, *fine!*" (The door slams.)

He sighs as he slowly walks out to the car. "Just once, I wish I could enjoy the day. Oh well . . ."

You can choose to be the gray cloud that hangs over your husband's head all day long and makes him dread coming home at the end of the day. (Which is why some men stop at a bar on the way home—they need fortitude to face what they know is coming. How sad!) Or you can choose to be the ray of sunshine that brightens his whole day. You can be the reason why, when the workday is over, he chooses not to hang out with the guys—because he can't wait to see you. He looks forward to telling you about his day, seeing your face beam when he tells you about the big compliment he got from his boss, or the base hit, hole in one, or the impossible ball he got to on the tennis court.

If you encourage him, compliment him, and build his confidence, you'll get extra care and attention when he returns. Be interested in what he likes. It doesn't mean you have to participate. I could not play baseball. There are other things you can do together. Allow him to enjoy his "men" activities.

Let him know that you're happy he is able to do things he loves. It will delight him.

Delight

Every husband should delight in his wife, and look for ways to bring delight to her.

Delighting *In*

Proverbs 5:18, 19 says: "Let your wife be a fountain of blessing for you. Rejoice in the wife of your youth. She is a loving deer, a graceful doe. Let her breasts satisfy you always. May you always be captivated by her love."

One of the most important ways you can show your wife that you take delight in her is to let her know that you only have eyes for her.

Mostly, I'm talking about pornography. Men (and women), if you have pornographic material around the house, throw it away. If you look at sexually explicit Web sites, stop it. Viewing pornography can corrupt your sexuality and harm your marriage by making your partner feel that she isn't "woman enough" to satisfy you.

I know this is a difficult and embarrassing subject, but it's an important one. If you don't think so, listen to this:

- In a ChristiaNet survey of Christian adults, 50 percent of men and 20 percent of women said they are addicted to pornography.[4]
- Pastors.com surveyed over 1,300 pastors and found that over half (54 percent) had visited an Internet porn site at some time during the past twelve months.
- In a similar survey commissioned by *Christianity Today*, one-third of pastors said they had visited a sexually explicit Web site.

Here are a few more chilling statistics:

- At $13.3 billion annually, the porn industry in the United States brings in more money than the NFL, NBA, and Major League Baseball combined.
- In a survey of five Christian colleges, 48 percent of the male students admitted using pornography.

Ruth and I believe that pornography is one of the key reasons that so many marriages today are failing. According to an article by Dr. Mark A. Yarhouse in *Christian Counseling Today* magazine, 42 percent of adults said that their partner's use of pornography made them feel insecure. And an MSNBC poll found that as many as 80 percent of visitors to sex sites were spending so much time on the Internet that they were putting their real-life relationships at risk.

It seems incredible to me that a man would choose fantasy sex over the real thing with his wife, as God intended. But based on what women have told me after hearing me speak on the topic of marriage, I know it's true. Tears spilled down the cheeks of one lovely young woman who told me, "I always go to bed alone. My husband stays in his office, looking at pornography on the Internet. He hasn't touched me in months."

> One of the most important ways you can show your wife that you take delight in her is to let her know that you only have eyes for her.

Something is wrong with this picture!

If you are a regular viewer of porn, or if you're tempted to look at porn, remember that Jesus said anyone who looks at a woman in a lustful way is committing adultery in his heart (Matthew 5:28). The Bible also says: "God's will is for you to be holy, so stay away from all sexual sin. Then each of you will control his own body and live in holiness and honor—not in lustful passion like the pagans who do not know God and his ways" (1 Thessalonians 4:3-5).

Proverbs 6:27-29 asks some great questions: "Can a man scoop a flame into his lap and not have his clothes catch on fire? Can he walk on hot coals and not blister his feet? So it is with the man who sleeps with another man's wife. He who embraces her will not go unpunished."

About twenty years ago, I had the great honor to be involved in a Billy Graham crusade at the Carrier Dome in Syracuse, New York. Although I'm almost never at a loss for words, I can't even begin to describe what a thrill it was to be on that stage while Billy Graham, George Beverly Shea, and Cliff Barrows shared the love of God with nearly fifty thousand people. I virtually floated out of that building on a spiritual high. I was filled to overflowing with God's love and power.

Even though it was late when I got back to my hotel room, I was too keyed up to sleep. Instead, I decided that I'd turn on the TV to catch some late news and check the NBA scores from around the country. As I headed past the TV to hang my jacket in the closet, I casually picked up the remote and clicked the TV on.

What in the world—

There on the screen, a young man and woman, completely nude, were engaged in sex.

I froze in my tracks.

The remote tumbled to the floor.

I couldn't believe what I was seeing.

As soon as I could get my brain to work, I bent down to grab the remote and changed the channel.

I didn't look at that X-rated movie very long. Five to ten seconds at most. Still, that wonderful spiritual high rushed out of me like air going out of a balloon. It wasn't that I was interested or aroused. I was appalled more than anything.

At the same time, what I saw stuck in my mind. I had been brought back down to earth in just a matter of seconds. To me, that speaks of the great negative power of pornography, and how Satan uses it to hurt and destroy. Nothing good can come from viewing such degrading filth.

> Men, don't settle for an image on a screen or in a book when you have a real flesh-and-blood partner who committed to love you for the rest of her life.

I've had men tell me that they look at porn to whet their sexual appetite, so they can be better lovers for their wives. It simply doesn't work that way. Pornography creates a hunger for bizarre, unnatural sex, and it gets worse as time goes on. What thrilled the addict yesterday seems boring and commonplace today, so he is always looking for bigger kicks.

I read about a study in which rats were forced to choose between food and cocaine, and many chose cocaine. They were willing to starve to death in order to get their drug high. That's the way it is with men addicted to pornography. They are willing to starve themselves and their marriages in order to get an artificial high. What a shame!

Men, don't settle for an image on a screen or in a book when you have a real flesh-and-blood partner who committed to love you for the rest of her life. Get your head out of a fantasy world and take a look at the beautiful creature God gave you. As the great Roman philosopher Cicero said, "A man would have no pleasure in discovering all the beauties of the universe, even in heaven itself, unless he had a partner to whom he might communicate his joys."[5]

The Bible says, "Didn't the LORD make you one with your wife? In body and spirit you are his. . . . So guard your heart; remain loyal to the wife of your youth" (Malachi 2:15). Show your spouse that you take delight in her, and she will take delight in you!

Bringing Delight *To*

It's also important to bring delight to your spouse. In order to do this, you have to know what she wants. Think you know your mate well? Let's find out. In the left margin, use a pencil to rank the following actions from 1 to 10 (1 being top) according to how much each would delight her:

- Send her flowers just to let her know you love her.
- Take her out for a romantic dinner at her favorite restaurant.
- Help her with the housework.
- Give her a back rub.
- Spend a quiet evening together at home, talking about issues that are important to both of you.
- Tell her that you'll stay home and babysit the kids so she can have an evening out with her friends.
- Plan a surprise weekend getaway.
- Take her shopping and help her pick out a new dress (or two).
- Surprise her with tickets to a concert or play.
- Make a list of things that need to be done around the house and then get busy doing them.

Done? OK, now cover your answers, give the list to your wife, and ask her to rank the options from 1 to 10.

When she's finished, compare notes and see if you knew her as well as you thought you did. (By the way, maybe you'll want to turn the tables and have her draw up a list for you. Remember that a great marriage is one in which both partners invest 100 percent of themselves into the relationship.)

> Remember that a great marriage is one in which both partners invest 100 percent of themselves into the relationship.

In his wonderful book *The Five Love Languages*, Dr. Gary Chapman points out that various people have different ways of showing and receiving love. He says, "My conclusion after twenty years of marriage counseling is that there are basically five emotional love languages—five ways that people speak and understand emotional love."[6]

These five love languages are:

- words of affirmation
- quality time
- receiving gifts
- acts of service
- physical touch[7]

In other words, some of us show our love through words of affirmation or by performing acts of service. Others express love best through physical touch, giving gifts, or by spending quality time with the one they love.

Problems can arise in a marriage when the husband and wife don't speak the same love language.

Dr. Chapman puts it this way: "Seldom do a husband and wife have the same primary emotional love language. We tend to speak our primary love language, and we become confused when our spouse does not understand what we are communicating. We are expressing our love, but the message does not come through because we are speaking what, to them, is a foreign language."[8]

I mentioned earlier that one of the ways I show my love for Ruth is through acts of service, like preparing a grapefruit for her breakfast and running her bathwater at the end of the day. I know Ruth well enough to understand that these simple acts touch her heart and please her.

But what if Ruth most needed from me words of love and affirmation that I never gave? In that case, my small acts of service wouldn't mean nearly as much to her.

I'd be thinking, *What's wrong with her? I do all these things for her, and she doesn't even seem to notice.*

And she'd be thinking, *What's wrong with him? He does all these things for me, but he refuses to give me what I really need.*

If you want your marriage to be strong and healthy, you must show your love in a way that is meaningful to your spouse. If you don't know what that is, ask her.

By the way, if you discover that what your spouse really wants from you is physical touch, that doesn't mean you should skip things like acts of service, gifts, and words of affirmation. All are important ways of demonstrating love. It's just that you want to put your main focus on whichever of these will mean the most—will bring delight—to her.

Now that you know what will encourage and delight your spouse, what are you waiting for? Get busy.

Reflect & Discuss

1. Do you feel that you can do a better job of encouraging your spouse? If so, how?

2. Is there one particular area in which your spouse is especially in need of your encouragement? How can you encourage and edify him or her in this area?

3. Is there one particular area in which you are especially in need of your spouse's encouragement? Have you expressed this need? If not, why not?

4. Were you startled by any of the statistics about pornography given in this chapter? If so, which ones? What was most alarming about them?

5. According to a Barna Research Group survey, 38 percent of Americans believe there is nothing wrong with viewing pornography.[9] Do you agree or disagree? Explain your answer. Then read Philippians 4:8 and 1 Thessalonians 4:3-5.

6. What steps can we take to reduce pornography's impact on American society?

7. What are some specific ways you "take delight" in your spouse?

8. Look back at the five love languages on page 88. What is your primary love language?

9. What is your spouse's primary love language?

10. Think of at least five things you will do within the next week that will bring delight to your spouse. Write them down; then follow through.

Teammates for Life

ALONE WE CAN DO SO LITTLE; TOGETHER WE CAN DO SO MUCH.

—HELEN KELLER

H as anything like this ever happened to you?

On a clear, crisp Saturday afternoon in late fall, Tom found himself at the shopping mall with his wife, Caroline, who was looking for a couple of new winter outfits. He was trying his best to appear cheerful and upbeat, but the truth was that he hated shopping and, about twenty minutes into the experience, was more than ready to head for home.

Caroline was having trouble finding exactly what she was looking for and had been through two stores without making a purchase. As they were about to enter store number three, she said, "Hon, I know this isn't any fun for you. Why don't we split up for a while? We can meet in, say, an hour and fifteen minutes at the fountain?"

"You don't mind?"

"Of course not. Why would I mind?"

Tom happily agreed, and headed off in the direction of the nearest electronics store, where he had fun checking out the latest gadgetry. After that, he headed to the bookstore, where he spent some time browsing the shelves.

The next thing he knew, it was nearly time to meet his wife. That's when the panic hit.

Where were they supposed to meet?

He had no idea. He hadn't been listening!

At the mall entrance? No, that didn't sound right.

At the food court? That didn't ring a bell.

He reached into his pocket for his cell phone so he could call her, but it wasn't there. He must have left it on his desk at home.

The only thing he could do was walk the length of the mall, trying to spot her in the midst of the Saturday afternoon crowd.

Now if this were a ghost story, I'd tell you that Tom is still roaming the halls of that mall, swinging an old railroad lantern back and forth, and calling out Caroline's name. Fortunately for Tom, it's not quite that bad. He finally found her, sitting on a bench near the fountain in the center of the mall, and he was only thirty-five minutes late.

His dear, sweet wife was not a happy camper.

"What happened?" she demanded. "I was afraid something happened to you!"

He couldn't think of any decent excuses, so he told the truth. "I'm sorry, but . . . I couldn't remember where I was supposed to meet you."

"Couldn't remember, or . . ."

He sighed. "OK. I guess I wasn't listening."

At this point, we'd better let Tom and Caroline have their privacy. Things are going to get just a little heated. This was not the first time Tom had tuned out his wife in mid-sentence, and Caroline was getting tired of it.

Unfortunately, Tom has lots of company. Two related complaints that I hear over and over again from women are:

- My husband doesn't listen to me.
- My husband doesn't talk to me about what's going on in his life.

Those two points cover the essence of being involved. And *involve* is the *I* in *edify*.

Involved Means Listening

Even though it is generally the husband who doesn't listen, this is not a husbands-only problem. Some men are terrific listeners and don't have any problem sharing their innermost thoughts and feelings with their partners. But as is true with everything else in this book, the most important thing you can do is ask yourself, "Am I like this?" And if so, "How can I change? What steps can I take to help build the BEST possible marriage?"

Do you remember a time when you and your spouse never grew tired of listening to each other? Before you were married, you would talk on the phone for hours and never want to say good-bye. What happened? Do you need to rediscover the pleasure of conversation with the one you love? Far too many of us are like Johnny, the third grader who didn't seem to hear a word his teacher said.

"Johnny," she finally asked, "do you have a hearing problem?"

"No ma'am," the child replied. "I have a listening problem."

Men like Johnny, who struggle with a listening problem, don't mean to be hurtful. Yet the message they send is that they really don't care.

I've got to admit, I'm not always the best listener. I'm a high-energy guy, and sometimes my mind moves on before the conversation is finished. When that happens, I have to slow down and pull myself back to the present. Occasionally, I even admit that I wasn't listening and ask Ruth to repeat something she just told me. That can be embarrassing, but it's better than pretending I heard what she said when I really don't have a clue.

I could also do a better job of sharing my feelings. Society has reinforced the notion that it isn't manly to get in touch with our emotions and share our feelings. But the truth is that stuffing your feelings can lead to a host of illnesses—and destroy your marriage.

Listening and sharing openly are important components of teamwork, which is something every marriage needs.

One of my jobs, as senior vice president of the NBA's Orlando Magic, is assessing talent so we can put the best possible team on the court. We need just the right mix of players: good ball handlers, guys who can shoot the lights out from three-point range, big centers who can block shots and grab rebounds, and so on. You also have to have a strong bench—backup players who can come into the game when your starters need a break, or to add some energy when things are getting a little lackluster out there.

It's also important to recognize talent that others may pass up, finding the hidden jewels that are not yet demanding multimillion dollar contracts in order to keep your payroll under the salary cap.

> Talent certainly helps a team win ball games, but good chemistry is just as important. Teams tend to win when there is real communication and involvement.

In professional sports, the teams with the best talent do not always win championships. A few years ago, nearly everyone expected the Los Angeles Lakers to win the NBA championship. They had a roster full of future Hall of Famers—arguably the best team in the history of professional basketball. Yet they fell short because those superstars did not gel into a cohesive unit. Over the last few years, the New York Yankees have consistently had the highest payroll (and thus it would seem, the best collection of talent) in Major League Baseball, but they have not gone to the World Series.

Talent certainly helps a team win ball games, but good chemistry is just as important. Teams tend to win when there is real communication and involvement, where the players know each other well enough to anticipate each others' moves.

Sometimes I go into a team's clubhouse before a game and see a bunch of guys doing their own thing. This one is over in the corner with his cell phone. That one has his earphones on. Another is reading a book, and so on. There's no friendly banter going on. It's clear that these guys aren't involved with each other, and I know right away that no matter how much individual talent they may have, they're never going to be a great team.

The Boston Celtics' great center Bill Russell once told me, "I could have scored more, but it would have taken energy away from playing defense. We always won as a team, not individuals, and basketball is a team game. One man can't win it."

And another legend, UCLA's Coach John Wooden, put it this way: "Ten strong field horses could not pull an empty baby carriage if they worked independently of each other."[1]

The Bible says of teamwork, "Two are better than one, because they have a good return for their work: If one falls down, his friend can help him up. But pity the man who falls and has no one to help him up! Also, if two lie down together, they will keep warm. But how can one keep warm alone? Though one may be overpowered, two can defend themselves. A cord of three strands is not quickly broken" (Ecclesiastes 4:9-12, *NIV*).

Don't isolate yourself from your spouse. Involve her in your life by listening to what's on her heart and sharing what's on yours. Most human beings do a pretty poor job of listening. We don't listen because we're too busy thinking about what we're going to say next, or because we let our minds wander back to something that happened yesterday. A failure to listen is always harmful, but especially so in a marriage.

Ernest Hemingway said, "I like to listen. I have learned a great deal from listening carefully. Most people never listen."[2]

Here are a few simple things we husbands can do to improve our listening skills and be more involved:

Look Your Spouse in the Eye When She's Talking to You

Making eye contact helps you to stay focused. Just as important, it shows your spouse that you are concentrating on her and listening to what she's saying. If your eyes glaze over, or she sees that you're focused on what's going on fifty feet behind her, she's going to get the feeling that you're not really tuned in.

Maintain Focus

The best way you can do this is to avoid doing two things at once. Don't try to read the newspaper or balance your checkbook while your wife is talking to you. When you're in the middle of a conversation, keep your mind on the conversation. If you find your thoughts starting to wander off somewhere, catch them and bring them back. Poor listening is a bad habit, and like all bad habits, it can be broken.

Pay Attention to Body Language

Smiles. Frowns. Grimaces. Shrugs. All of these things can tell you as much as words can. A facial expression or a wave of the hand can make all the difference in the world. Something can sound angry or defensive, but the smile on the speaker's face will tell you that it's all in jest. A good listener uses his ears *and* his eyes.

Don't Be Afraid of Silence

You don't have to fill every bit of air space. Sometimes, the best communication between a husband and wife takes place when they are just sitting in silence with each other. There are few things as wonderful as a comfortable silence. An online article out of Great Britain was titled "The Horror of a Silent Holiday." Though that might sound like it's about spending Christmas alone after having lost a loved one, it's not. It's about avoiding awkward silences while on outings with your partner. The whole piece focused on this "horror" but, at the very end, admitted: "Few things can beat the comfortable silence that couples can share together. You can enjoy just being together on the beach or when you're admiring the sunset. The companionable silence of couples who feel totally at ease together is wonderful."[3]

Sometimes, a silence can be worth more than a thousand words. Or ten thousand.

Let Her Know You Hear Her

Let your wife know that you're listening by asking questions, by nodding, or rephrasing what she said. Suppose you had an employee who always averted eye contact, mumbled one-word answers to your questions, and generally seemed to be disinterested in anything you had to say. You probably wouldn't nominate that person for Employee of the Year, would you? More than likely, he would soon be taking his place in the line at the unemployment office.

How do you think your boss would act if you treated him or her this way? Yet this is exactly how some people treat their spouses. They respond to anything their mates say with a snippy, sarcastic tone. They sigh, or roll their eyes, and act as if it's a bother to show their wives the time of day. If you catch yourself leaning in the wrong direction on any of these things, it's time for a change. One's life partner deserves as much courtesy and respect as he gives his boss.

Concerning courtesy and respect, here are three rules every husband should know and follow:

1. Never, ever, raise your voice to your wife—unless the house is on fire.
2. If you feel that you absolutely must criticize her or say something negative to her, do it gently and in love.
3. If you have to choose between making yourself look good and making her look good, choose her!

After all, you're teammates!

Don't Give Solutions Unless Your Spouse Asks for Them

Sometimes a woman just wants a listening ear. She wants her husband to understand how she's feeling about something and to empathize without passing judgment or trying to solve all of her problems.

Somebody clipped the following out of a newsletter and sent it to me. I've tried, unsuccessfully, to find out who wrote it. Whoever it was spoke on behalf of thousands of married women:

> When I ask you to listen and you start giving advice, you have not done what I have asked. When I ask you to listen and you begin to tell me why I shouldn't feel the way I do, you are trampling on my feelings. When I ask you to listen and you feel you have to do something to solve my problems, you have failed me, strange as it may seem. Listen. All I asked you to do was listen; not talk or do. Just hear me. I can do for myself. I am not helpless. When you do something for me that I need to do for myself, you contribute to my fear and weakness. But when you accept as fact that I feel what I feel, no matter how irrational, I can stop trying to convince you and get on with understanding what's behind that irrational feeling. And when that's clear, the answer will be obvious and I won't need any advice.

RUTH SAYS

Pat is a very good listener—when he can focus. I truly believe, although he has never been officially diagnosed, that Pat
has ADD or ADHD. (I never can remember the difference; but I
do know that both are connected to being hyper, and that's Pat.)
He always has to be busy. He *must* have goals to strive for. He
cannot sit and do nothing. There is a purpose to everything that
he does. Knowing that about him, I know that if I truly want him
to listen, I have to say things like:

- "Honey, do you have a minute to listen to me?"
- "Sweetheart, would you put that book down for a moment?
  I need your opinion."
- "Darlin', something is bothering me about a client, and I
  know you can probably help. Would you hear me out?"

Whenever I use one of these statements, he'll drop what he's
doing and listen. But first, I have to make an announcement that
it's really important.

Like the man in the mall, if people (men or women) are dis-
tracted, they may not really hear you, much less listen. So when
you want to be listened to, ask in a way that will cause the other
person, especially your spouse, to drop what he or she is doing
and focus on you.

It's not that people, even friends and other family members
including your spouse, don't want to listen to you. At the moment, they just don't realize how important it is to you. But when
you tell them, they will listen. It's like the classic line from *Field
of Dreams*: "If you build it, they will come."

So tell your sweetheart what you need. Once he gets it, he
will listen.

Involved Means Talking

Listening to your wife is only half of the equation. It's also important to talk to her. She loves you and wants to be your partner and helper, which is what God designed her to be (Genesis 2:18). If you shut her out, you are not only hurting her, but yourself as well.

I wouldn't dream of making an important decision without discussing it with Ruth first. She almost always helps me see the situation from an angle I hadn't considered. She's wise. Compassionate. Honest. And because of her, I've come to believe that there is such a thing as women's intuition. Most of all, I know that she is the partner God gave me, and he expects me to fully involve her in whatever is going on in my life.

I once heard best-selling author Kevin Leman talking on the radio about the best piece of advice he ever received—a few simple words from Dr. James Dobson: "Before you do anything," Dobson said, "run it past your wife."

> I know that she is the partner God gave me, and he expects me to fully involve her in whatever is going on in my life.

Now there's a man who knows what he's talking about.

One Sunday morning our associate pastor, Dr. Jimmy Knott, preached on the subject of marriage and communication. He said something funny that really hit home with me in a serious way: "Most of us men married the Holy Spirit, but we don't have the sense to listen to it."

The audience laughed and you could see men's heads nodding affirmatively all over the congregation. I turned and looked at Ruth's smiling face, gave her a high five, and said, "He's right."

She said, "Yes, I know."

There are two important questions I ask myself on a regular basis. The first is "What would Jesus do?" The second is "What would Ruth say?" As a Christian, I certainly don't want to do anything that is contrary to the spirit of Christ. As a relatively intelligent guy, I don't want to do anything that Ruth would find questionable or inadvisable. If I know in advance that Ruth is going to have a problem with something, or that it's going to take a bit of explaining on my part, I think twice about moving ahead.

I can't overstate it because it's so important: let your wife know what's going on in your world, and listen to what she says.

The late Randy Pausch (whose diagnosis of pancreatic cancer and book, *The Last Lecture*, put him in the international spotlight) told the story of his boss's insistence that people be able to contact Randy during his honeymoon.

Here's the message Randy put on his voice mail: "Hi, this is Randy. I waited until I was 39 to get married, so my wife and I are going away for a month. I hope you don't have a problem with that, but my boss does. Apparently, I have to be reachable."

Then he gave his wife's parents' names and their city and said, "If you call directory assistance, you can get their phone number. And then, if you can convince my in-laws that your emergency merits interrupting their only daughter's honeymoon, they have our number."

They didn't get any calls.[4]

Though Randy's life was cut short, this story he left us vividly illustrates that a marriage creates a new team. And while couples don't cut themselves off from involvement with others (except during the honeymoon!), the marriage must be given top priority.

Reflect **&** Discuss

1. How do you rate yourself as an involved teammate in the area of listening—good, fair, or poor? Explain your answer.

2. When was the last time you got into trouble because you didn't listen to your spouse? What happened, and what did you learn from that experience?

3. Read James 1:19. What three things are we told to do? Why is this good advice?

4. What practical steps can you take to improve your listening skills—especially in regard to your spouse?

5. Read Proverbs 1:5 in several Bible versions. How can listening "add to [your] learning"? (*NIV*).

6. How do you rate yourself as an involved teammate in the area of talking— good, fair, or poor? Explain your answer.

7. What aspects of communication are you and your spouse good at?

8. Where are the problem areas in your communication with your spouse?

9. What concrete steps can you take to be more of a team player in these areas?

Bringing Out the Best

IT IS THE NATURE OF MAN TO RISE TO GREATNESS IF GREATNESS IS EXPECTED OF HIM.

—JOHN STEINBECK

Grant Hill is one of my favorite basketball players. I loved him when he played for the Orlando Magic. And I still love him now that he's wearing the uniform of the Phoenix Suns. Grant had some injury problems during his time with the Magic, but he handled everything with patient good humor and remained one of the game's true gentlemen. A seven-time all-star, he also won the 2004–2005 NBA Sportsmanship Award for "sportsmanship, ethical behavior, fair play, and integrity."

I'll always treasure a letter I received from one of our fans after a game in December 2005: "I want to thank Grant Hill for being so gracious to the children at the Orlando Magic game," it said. "They had children lined up to greet the players as they came onto the court. Most of the players rushed by. Grant Hill stopped, smiled, and spoke to several of the children, including one of mine. He noticed my son had his safety patrol badge on and told him, 'Wow! You're a safety patrol? That's a cool job. Keep up the good work!' My son was on cloud nine."

Like I said, Grant's a classy guy.

During his college days, Grant played ball for the legendary Coach K—Mike Krzyzewski (you can see why they call him Coach K)—at Duke University. Grant said that when he first arrived at Duke, he was awestruck, and wondered if he could live up to expectations.

"I thought I wasn't good enough to play at Duke," he said, "that I was in over my head. But Coach K always felt I was better than I ever believed I could be. He constantly reassured me I would be something special. It took a while for me to believe in myself, but he always believed in me . . . and helped me gain the confidence I needed to make it to the NBA.

> It's so important to have someone say, "I believe in you."

"I wish I could go back and relive that experience. I wish I could be a freshman at that first meeting in the team locker room. I wish I could look into Coach K's eyes and hear him tell me, once again, that I was something special."

Grant Hill had tremendous natural talent, but without someone like Coach K to inspire and encourage him, that talent might have remained unfulfilled and undiscovered. We all need someone who encourages us to reach for our dreams. Sometimes it seems to me that the world is filled with negative people who are always anxious to criticize and tear others down. I suppose that sounds a bit cynical. It's just that we get more than enough negativity and criticism. That's why it's so important to have someone say, "I believe in you."

As we continue discussing the need to edify your spouse, let's talk about what it means to help your partner fulfill his or her greatest potential. The *F* in *edify* is for *fulfill*.

Fulfill—What It Means

I believe that God has given every person on this planet something to do that nobody else can accomplish. It may be something great; it may be something that seems insignificant to us—but is great to God, who doesn't see things the way we do.

It is my duty, as Ruth's husband, to help her find and fulfill God's plan for her. And it's her duty, as my wife, to help me find and fulfill the plan God has for me. I want to do everything within my power to help her fulfill every bit of her God-given potential. I can't be jealous of any success that comes her way. A marriage is not competition. I think that's one of the primary reasons why so many Hollywood marriages fail. Husbands and wives are competing for the spotlight rather than being delighted by each other's successes.

I know it can be difficult for a man to step aside and let his wife shine. I suppose that's because it's the nature of the male to want to provide for and protect his woman. It's the way God made us. Underneath their civilized facade, most men have a "Me Tarzan, you Jane" attitude. We're supposed to be bigger, stronger, more heroic. For this reason, it can be rough on a man's psyche when his wife makes more money than he does, has a better job than he does, or surpasses him in any other endeavor. We think we can run faster, shoot straighter, drive better, and get a quicker grasp on complicated issues. (Sorry, ladies, but that's just how we are, and it can be painful when you prove us wrong.)

I'm sure you've heard the old saying "Behind every good man, there's a good woman." That's the stereotype. The man succeeds while the woman stays quietly in the background, content to be the wind beneath his wings. But it's not always the case. Nor should it be.

Every wife should have her husband's unlimited encouragement and support as she strives to fulfill her God-given potential. And in case you're looking for a good role

> Most men have a "Me Tarzan, you Jane" attitude.

model, I've got one: Joseph, the husband of Mary and stepfather of Jesus. I can imagine a conversation like this one, at a party to welcome Joseph and Mary to the neighborhood:

"So, Joseph, what do you do for a living?"

"I'm a carpenter."

"A carpenter, huh? Say, can I have one of your business cards? I've been thinking about doing a little remodeling."

"Sure. Here you go. Let me know when you want to get started, and I'll come over and give you an estimate."

"Great! . . . And that's your wife over there?"

"Yes, that's Mary."

"She seems very pleasant. What does she do?"

"Oh, she's the mother of the Savior of the world."

"The . . . wha—?"

"The mother of the Savior of the world. You know, the Prince of Peace. Lord of lords. King of kings . . ."

Perhaps Joseph never had a conversation like the one I've just imagined. But he could have. I wonder what it was like for him to know that the woman he married had been chosen to be the mother of God's only begotten Son? It must have been hard for him to be proud of even his most beautiful and intricate work. How could being even the best cabinet crafter begin to compare with being the mother of Christ?

Yet Joseph fulfilled his own role with grace and bravery. He stood beside Mary when she became pregnant before they were married. He protected and comforted her on the long journey from Nazareth to Bethlehem. It's not that far by today's standards. Only about seventy miles. But there were no expressways in those days—only narrow, twisted, dusty paths across the hilly landscape. (And Mary was nine months pregnant.) After Jesus' birth, there was the much longer trip into Egypt to escape Herod's murderous plot. After that, the Bible doesn't say much about Joseph. He appeared again, briefly, when Jesus was twelve years old, but that's the last we hear of him.

> The woman he married had been chosen to be the mother of God's only begotten Son.

I wish I knew more about Joseph. The Bible assures us that he was a good, or righteous, man (Matthew 1:19), but he was more than that. He stands as a role model and example for every man who's ever married a high-achieving woman.

Fulfill—How to Do It

Let's talk briefly about some of the specific areas in which a woman needs her husband's support in order to grow and thrive, to be fulfilled.

Finances

I hope this doesn't sound old-fashioned. Today, more and more women are taking charge of their own financial future. They make their own investment decisions. They know all about the stock market, mutual funds, treasury bills, and money markets. The very idea that a husband would make all the financial decisions for his family seems like a relic from a bygone era. And yet I know there are still many women who would just as soon step aside and let their husbands take care of things. Even if your wife is among this group, please don't keep her in the dark about financial matters. Marriage is a partnership, and both partners need full financial disclosure. Women tend to live longer than men. Please make sure your wife is well prepared and knows exactly what to do if the Lord should call you home.

> **Make sure you have people on your team who can do things you can't do.**

Incidentally, I believe that both the husband and wife should play to each other's strengths. In the Williams household, Ruth takes care of all financial matters. I recognized early on that she had that gift and I did not. She takes care of paying all the bills, tithing to our church, contributing to issues involving our children and grandchildren, and giving to causes we want to support. She does it all—except investing.

In the very beginning she said, "I can handle the day-to-day finances and expenses, but I'm not an investment expert by any stretch of the imagination." Then she shared something with me. Years ago she had read in a Napoleon Hill book an idea that made a deep impression on her. The principle stated how important it is to surround oneself with capable people. Ruth shares this in every leadership seminar she does. It's a great rule to live by and especially to lead by.

It simply means that all of us are good at *some* things, but no one is good at *everything.* So when you're building a team, whether at work or at home, make sure you have people on your team who can do things you can't do. Ruth lives by this principle.

One of the first things she did after we were married was to build our team. I call them the Magnolia Mafia because Ruth is definitely "magnolia" through and through, and the team is made up entirely of women.

Before we make any major financial decisions, we consult our financial adviser, Janet. She eats and breathes investments, IRAs, pensions, and so forth.

We trust her completely, knowing that she's never steered us wrong and has our best interests at heart. We'd be foolish not to listen to her wise advice. My male ego does not require that I take charge in this area.

Two of our married daughters, Stephanie and Andrea, have husbands, Matt and Tracy, who love to cook and fix all the meals. Nowhere is it written that the wife has to do all the cooking. Both men have been trained professionally and know what they're doing in the kitchen. They are both wonderful cooks. I know because I've gotten to sample their recipes. In a good marriage, both partners are willing to let the other shine in the areas where he or she is strongest— whether it's finances or cooking.

Career

I would love it if every woman could stay home and take care of her family full-time. But these days it takes two incomes for most families just to get by. This is especially true in the early days of a marriage, when a couple is just beginning to find their financial footing.

It's ironic, but many families don't reach the point where the wife could stay home to take care of the children until the children are grown up! Besides, many women simply wouldn't find fulfillment in being a full-time homemaker. That's not the desire God has placed in their hearts. He has given them talents and abilities they can use to build a successful full-time career.

> What a tragedy it would be if women had to go around dumbing themselves down to keep their husbands happy.

Does your wife have a career? Does she *want* to have a career? Do you encourage her toward the fulfillment of her dreams in this area? She needs your support.

Is it true that most men are intimidated by strong, intelligent, capable women? I certainly hope not. Every husband should want his wife to be everything she's capable of being. What a tragedy it would be if women had to go around dumbing themselves down to keep their husbands happy.

Ruth is a trainer and consultant with the very prestigious FranklinCovey company, while at the same time working on her doctorate—and I couldn't be more proud of her. I am not threatened in the least by Ruth's success, because I know she has tremendous potential in these areas, and I want to see her achieve her potential to the fullest.

If you feel threatened by your spouse's achievements, ask God to help you with your attitude. Encourage your spouse to live her life to the fullest. She shouldn't have to play down and limit herself to 60 percent of her potential. It's just not fair.

RUTH SAYS

Pat is the master of this one. He's my biggest cheerleader. He's very proud of what I do and encourages me to do my best. He even helps me.

As he's reading his myriad of books, he often sees stories or quotes that he thinks might fit into one of my speeches. He copies them and brings them to me with statements like, "Hey, read this. Can you use this in 7 Habits?" Or, "Wow! Honey, look what I found . . . perfect for your time-management seminar." Or, "Sweetheart, read this. It fits great with leadership."

And when one of his stories or quotes makes it into one of my presentations, he shouts a great big "Yes!" He wants me to do well and he wants to be part of my success. Believe me, I appreciate that. Traveling these days is not as much fun as it used to be. Knowing I have Pat's support—and help—means a lot and takes some of the tension away.

When I get discouraged or tired, he's there to boost my spirits. When I'm writing and get to a point where I'm stuck, I can say, "I need help here. Read this and tell me what it needs." He will drop everything and give it his full attention. Many times we start bouncing ideas off each other and come up with something brilliant. Then we high-five each other and hug.

Relationships

Every wife needs other women to talk to, so every husband should encourage his wife to have friends. Tell her you'll stay home with the kids once a month (or more if you can) so she can go out to dinner or play Bunco with her girlfriends.

I've known men who were jealous of their wives' girlfriends. They didn't want their wives to spend any time on the phone when they were home. If their wives wanted a night out with the girls, they went into apoplexy. They must have mistakenly believed that one of the wedding vows was "Do you promise to forsake all your friends and lavish all your attention on your husband?" I do believe that a wife's first allegiance is to her husband and family, but God designed us for fellowship with other people—and especially other believers.

RUTH SAYS

One of the greatest rewards in parenting (other than having grandchildren) is building friendships with your adult children. If you've built a solid parenting relationship as they grow up (and we'll talk about that later), then children become friends as adults. Parents, hear this clearly: I did *not* say be friends with your children as they are growing up. Young children need parents, not friends. But once they reach independence and are building their own lives, the relationship you've had as parent and child can blossom into a very close friendship.

Wives do need girlfriends. However, in my case, my children are now my friends. There is nothing more fun than spending time hanging out with my grown children. One of my favorite things is for my oldest daughter, Stephanie, to come over with her husband, Matt, and my grandson, Max. We take our boat and ride around the lake talking about issues of the day and life in general. Sometimes we end up at Houston's, a restaurant on the other side of the lake, sitting outside, having snacks and cold drinks.

I know I can confide in Stephanie, and she knows she can confide in me. She was always able to do that growing up, and now, as an adult and mom herself, she can still do that with confidence. We talk. We laugh. We cry. We debate. Spending time with Stephanie is the most fun "girl time" I have. And Stephanie is not the only one. Sometimes there are three or four kids and grandchildren and we just sit around and talk.

Be parents as your children are growing up. Once they become adults, the friendships are priceless!

The playwright Euripides hit the mark when he said, "It is a good thing to be rich, it is a good thing to be strong, but it is a better thing to be beloved of many friends."[1]

Spirituality

The man must take the role of spiritual leader in his home. His wife and children will follow. It's up to you to get the family up and off to church on Sunday morning. You're the one to lead the family in prayer at mealtime, bring everyone together for family devotions, and so forth. If you don't lead the way in spiritual matters, your wife will have to do it, and that's not what God intended. When the husband abdicates his intended spiritual role, chaos results.

> If you don't lead the way in spiritual matters, your wife will have to do it, and that's not what God intended.

Ruth and I were recently visiting with some good friends of ours, when the wife informed us that their oldest son was going through a divorce. Naturally, I expressed my regret, and said I hoped he and his wife would be able to work things out.

She shook her head. "I kind of think they're past that point." Then she said, "One of the reasons why this happened was because she wanted to go to church and he didn't."

"Really? Why didn't she just go without him?"

"Well, I guess he kind of sabotaged things. The whole family would get up and get dressed, but then when they were on their way to church, he'd say something to the kids like, 'Wouldn't you rather go to the breakfast buffet?'"

She sighed. "He really undermined her in this area, and I guess she got tired of it."

We sat in silence for a moment, as I thought about how often this sort of thing happens in a marriage.

Then the wife shot her husband a meaningful look. "You know, you did the same thing forty years ago when we first got married. I wanted to go to church, but you didn't—so I just gave up."

Her husband just sat there without saying a word. Forty years later, and she was still resentful that her husband had not taken his rightful role as spiritual leader of his family. Forty years later, and the consequences of his own actions were being felt in his son's faltering marriage.

The Bible says, "A husband is the head of his wife as Christ is the head of the church" (Ephesians 5:23). Fellas, you regulate the spiritual temperature in your household. This might seem ironic, since women are typically more sensitive to the things of the Spirit. Here are some ways you can encourage your wife to grow closer to the Lord and find spiritual fulfillment:

- Pray with and for her.
- Read the Bible together.
- Have regular family devotions.
- Get involved in a church where Christ is honored, if you're not involved in one already.
- Join a small group.
- Encourage her to take part in a women's Bible study.
- Read good Christian books together, and listen to Christian music during long trips in the car.

Perhaps you can think of some other fun ways you can both grow closer to the Lord, and therefore closer to each other.

Children

Parenting is more than a one-person job. (And sometimes, when my nineteen kids were growing up, I was tempted to think it was more than a two-person job.) If you have children, you and your wife must be in agreement with regard to things like discipline and expectations. It's also crucial for the husband to be involved in tasks like getting the children ready for school, making sure they do their homework, and seeing to it that they get to bed on time.

Each parent has a role to fulfill. In the Williams house, when the children were living at home, Ruth and I worked together to make sure our children kept their rooms neat, cleaned their bathrooms, put their laundry away, and so on. We do the same

> You and your wife must be in agreement with regard to things like discipline and expectations.

thing with our grandchildren now. (It's easier with grandchildren. They listen better. Ha!) However, sometimes it was a struggle. They didn't always do what we wanted the first time we asked. But Ruth and I always stood together, and I think that's one of the reasons why we've found so much enjoyment and fulfillment in being parents and grandparents.

RUTH SAYS

Pat and I have written about parenting before in our book *You've Got to Be Kidding*. We've done radio and TV interviews about parenting. Because of our family's unusual makeup, we have been written about in magazines and newspapers, so I don't want to overdo this topic. Nevertheless, there are a few things I'd like to pass on, especially to young parents:

Be the spiritual teachers of your children.
Read the Bible and Bible storybooks to them, and sing "Jesus Loves Me" to them and with them.

This past Thanksgiving, five-year-old Laila, our oldest grand-daughter, and her three-year-old cousin, Ava, asked to say the blessing at the table. Right before the meal, they came to me and whispered, "Grammy, can we get everyone to sing 'Jesus Loves Me' for the blessing?" I said, "Of course."

So I announced to the group of forty people (some immediate family and some of their extended families) that Laila and Ava were in charge of the blessing and they wanted everyone to sing "Jesus Loves Me." So that's what we did. Laila and Ava were so proud that they had learned the song and that everyone wanted to sing with them.

Get your children grounded in spiritual things early; take them to Sunday school and church every week. Let them see you and hear you praying, and pray with them every night before bed. When you talk about decisions, bring the Bible into it.

> I think I made fewer wrong decisions because of my parents' spiritual influence.

I am one of the fortunate ones, blessed beyond measure to have been born to my parents. Both of them are with Jesus now, but their teachings live on. My father was an honorable, loving, and godly man. My mother was a nurturing, loving, kind, and godly woman. They gave me the foundation of my faith, and I am forever grateful to them.

I can vividly remember bringing problems to my mother or father, who would bring me to Scripture and show me what God said about the situation. We would read it and discuss it together, and then they would ask me, "So what do you think you should do?" I couldn't help but make the right decision. Not that I never made the wrong one; I did, because that's part of being a teenager. But I think I made fewer wrong decisions because of my parents' spiritual influence.

Balance love with discipline.

I got lots of both from my parents. My mother would do special things for me when I was being "good." For example, I might come home from school and find on my bed—for no reason—the new sweater or shoes I'd been wanting.

After squealing in delight, I'd ask, "Mom, what's this for?"

"No reason. Just because I love you."

I found myself doing the exact same thing with our children, and now I do it with the grandchildren. It's fun to see the delighted smiles on their faces. It's part of loving, along with lots of hugs and kisses.

On the other side of the coin, my mother also punished me when I did something wrong. But I never went to bed without her telling me she loved me and knew I would do better from that point on.

> One of the most important things you can do for your children is to openly love your spouse.

Kids need and want—yes, *want*—discipline. It shows you care and want them to be better human beings. The type of discipline you use may vary with individual children because their personalities are different, but it is important that they all receive a just punishment for the same misbehavior.

Love each other.

One of the most important things you can do for your children is to openly love your spouse. It gives children a feeling of security and shows them how to love.

Earlier in the book, I mentioned a young woman who had a very controlling husband. The more I talked with her, the more I realized that her husband didn't know how to love. He had spent a lifetime with two parents who shouted and screamed at each other all the time. They cut each other down and rarely had any-thing nice to say about the other. They had stuck it out with each other, but had greatly damaged their son without even realizing it. I hope the two young people make it in their marriage, but I'm not very hopeful unless they get some counseling and he learns how to truly love her. Your children learn to love from you; make sure you're showing them how.

I hear wives (young and old alike) complain about the fact that their husbands travel, leaving them alone to take care of children and household chores. Some of them actually criticize their husbands to their children, saying things like, "If your fa-ther really loved us, he wouldn't leave us so much." This makes me sick for the kids.

As I was growing up, my father left home every Monday and returned every Friday. He traveled several southern states selling chain saws. He would call every Wednesday night to talk about our week so far and tell us he missed us and couldn't wait to get home on Friday. My brother and I knew he called at about the same time each Wednesday, and we would hover around the phone until he did.

When we complained that Daddy was always gone, my moth-er would say, "Daddy is working really hard for us. He doesn't like being away, but he has to so we can eat and you can have the things you want. Let's tell Daddy thank you for working so hard for us this weekend when he gets home. OK?"

We ran to him when he pulled in the driveway that Friday, jumping on him, kissing him, saying, "Thank you, Daddy, for working so hard for us." He gave us great big hugs, looked over our heads toward Mom, and smiled. That smile said thank you back to her, and it made his traveling easier.

Pat is away on some weekends, speaking at conventions or

preaching at a church somewhere. One day Laila said, "Grammy, Poppers is gone too much." And you know what I said? "Laila, Poppers is working really hard for us. So let's leave him a voice mail and tell him thank you."

And we did.

A loving, faithful spouse is one of God's greatest gifts. Wouldn't it be wonderful if every husband and wife lived as if they understood that—and then sought to love, nurture, and bring to fulfillment the best in each other? I'm reminded of this quote from Matthew Henry: "Eve was not taken out of Adam's head to top him, neither out of his feet to be trampled on by him, but out of his side to be equal with him, under his arm to be protected by him, and near his heart to be loved by him."[2]

> If you seek to bring out the best in your partner, you'll certainly bring out the BEST in your marriage.

If you seek to bring out the best in your partner, you'll certainly bring out the BEST in your marriage, and you just may find that "happily ever after" isn't something that only happens in fairy tales.

Reflect & Discuss

1. Read Ephesians 5:21-33. In what ways can you "submit to one another" by helping your spouse fulfill his or her God-given potential?

2. What do you think Paul meant when he wrote that the husband is the head of the wife?

3. Describe how you are living in obedience to this directive.

4. Do you think it's really possible for a man to love his wife as much as Christ loves the church? Why or why not?

5. In what tangible ways can you show Christlike love in your daily interactions with your spouse?

6. Are there specific areas where you could do a better job of supporting your spouse? If so, what are they, and how can you change your behavior in these areas?

7. Read 1 Corinthians 13:4. Would you say this verse describes your attitude toward your spouse? Why or why not?

8. How does it please you when your spouse is successful or when others honor her?

9. Does he or she know how you feel? Are you sure? If not, maybe it's time for you to tell your spouse.

Learning to Forgive

> *WE CANNOT LOVE UNLESS WE HAVE ACCEPTED FORGIVENESS, AND THE DEEPER OUR EXPERIENCE OF FORGIVENESS IS, THE GREATER IS OUR LOVE.*
>
> —PAUL TILLICH

When Nelson Mandela came to power in South Africa, he brought to trial many of those who had committed atrocities during the years of apartheid. Mandela's desire was justice rather than vengeance. Anyone who was willing to face his accusers and confess his guilt would not be punished.

One day an old woman was brought in to face the man accused of murdering her husband and her only son. When asked what she wanted from the killer, she said, "Although I have no family, I still have a lot of love to give." She told the court that she would like the accused to visit her regularly so she could treat him as her son. Then she requested that she could come forward and embrace the man so he would know that her forgiveness was real.

As the old woman made her way forward, the prisoner fainted, apparently overwhelmed by his own shame and her ability to love and forgive him despite what he had done.[1]

Forgiveness is unbelievably powerful.

You can really empower your marriage by living in a constant state of forgiveness toward each other. If you are serious about edifying your spouse, think of the *Y* in *edify* as standing for *yield*.

Yielding—What It Means

The late Corrie ten Boom, author of *The Hiding Place*, told of an amazing encounter that moves me almost to tears each time I hear it. Two years after World War II ended, she spoke in a church in Munich, Germany. At the end of her talk, she was startled to see a familiar face walking down the aisle in her direction. Although he was now dressed in civilian clothes, there was no mistaking him. The man had been a guard at the Nazi concentration camp Ravensbruck. Corrie and her sister, Betsie, had been imprisoned there for concealing Jews in their home during the Nazi occupation of Holland. Betsie had died in that camp. Now the former guard stood right in front of her.

> You can really empower your marriage by living in a constant state of forgiveness toward each other.

"You mentioned Ravensbruck in your talk," he was saying. "I was a guard there." No, he did not remember me.

"But since that time," he went on, "I have become a Christian. I know that God has forgiven me for the cruel things I did there, but I would like to hear it from your lips as well. Fräulein," again the hand came out—"will you forgive me?"

And I stood there—I whose sins had again and again to be forgiven —and could not forgive. . . .

It could not have been many seconds that he stood there—hand held out—but to me it seemed hours as I wrestled with the most difficult thing I had ever had to do.

For I had to do it—I knew that. The message that God forgives has a prior condition: that we forgive those who have injured us. . . .

"Help!" I prayed silently. "I can lift my hand. I can do that much. You supply the feeling."

And so woodenly, mechanically, I thrust my hand into the one stretched out to me. And as I did, an incredible thing took place. The current started in my shoulder, raced down my arm, sprang into our joined hands. And then this healing warmth seemed to flood my whole being, bringing tears to my eyes.

"I forgive you, brother!" I cried. "With all my heart!"

For a long moment we grasped each other's hands, the former guard and the former prisoner. I had never known God's love so intensely, as I did then.[2]

It's kind of hard to be angry with your spouse about something after reading a story like that. Every person on this planet lives in constant need of forgiveness, and this is especially true of husbands and wives. On the TV game show *Family Feud*, contestants were asked, "Name the person who knows how to push your buttons." The number one answer? Of course, "My spouse."

Sad, but true. We know how to hit each other where it hurts, and that's what we do. Instead, we should live as described by James, the brother of Jesus: "The wisdom from above is first of all pure. It is also peace loving, gentle at all times, and willing to *yield* to others. It is full of mercy and good deeds" (James 3:17, emphasis added).

> "The wisdom from above is first of all pure. It is also peace loving, gentle at all times, and willing to *yield* to others."

A wise teacher once taught her high school students a wonderful lesson about forgiveness. When they arrived in her class one morning, they saw that her desk was covered with potatoes. Imagine their murmured surprise. What was going on? Had their favorite teacher suddenly lost her mind?

Not quite.

As she handed out a plastic bag to each of her pupils, she told them, "I want you to take a few moments to think about the people who've done you wrong. People you just can't forgive." Next, she told them to come forward and get a potato for every person they'd thought of.

"Now write each name on a potato, date it, and put it in the bag I gave you."

Every student took at least one potato. Some took four or five potatoes. As you can imagine, their sacks were quite heavy.

The teacher then instructed her students to take their sacks of potatoes with them everywhere they went for the next week. They were to carry them from class to class during the day, put them on the floor by their beds at night, and never let them out of their sight.

This was a terrible inconvenience, of course. And over time, the potatoes began to rot and decay, leaving behind a nasty, smelly slime.

Through their teacher, these young men and women learned to let go of the grudges they had carried around for so long. They understood something of the price we pay when we refuse to forgive. I'm not suggesting that you go out and buy your spouse a sack of potatoes, or that you start carrying potatoes around with you. But do remember this old Amish proverb: "Forgiveness is as valuable to the one forgiven as to the one who forgives."

Here are some terrific words to live by, from the pen of that great American poet, Anonymous:

> I found a little remedy
> to ease the life we live
> and make the day a happier one:
> it is the word "forgive."

Yielding—How It Plays Out

How can you learn to live in a yielded, forgiving state? How can you forgive when the person who has vowed to cherish and honor you has treated you in a thoughtless, hurtful way?

My friend Mark Atteberry said, "Apologizing is hard. But this is where you stand to gain a degree of peace and reclaim your self-respect. . . . You need to apologize if at all possible. You can't go back and undo the damage your razor-sharp tongue and hot temper may have caused, but by doing the hard thing, you give God something he can work with."[3]

Over thirty years ago, the late Jamie Buckingham wrote a book called *Risky Living*. My copy has seen better days. It's a bit dog-eared, and some of the pages have come out of the binding. But I hang onto it because it's full of wisdom like this: "I discovered how to tell a person you forgive them. You do it by telling them you love them. Genuine forgiveness will always manifest itself in love. In fact, if it doesn't cause you to love the person forgiven, there is good reason to doubt the sincerity and genuineness of your forgiveness. You love because you forgive. Forgiveness is an act of the will. Love is the result. . . . The way to say, 'I forgive you,' is to say, 'I love you.'"[4]

You might be thinking, *But aren't there times when forgiveness just isn't possible?*

Yes—and no.

There are times when reconciling is simply not advisable or safe. Ruth and I both know individuals who have undergone terrible physical or emotional abuse—or perhaps both. After talking to counselors and pastors, it has become evident that victims can forgive *without* rebuilding a relationship. Some relationships simply must be abandoned because it would be dangerous to stay in them.

> Some relationships simply must be abandoned because it would be dangerous to stay in them.

No one should put himself or herself in harm's way. Whether it's a beaten and abused wife, or a child emotionally deprived and physically or sexually mistreated, one cannot—and should not—have contact with the abuser, even if it's a parent or other family member. Rare is the case in which the abuser seeks help, asks forgiveness, and turns his behavior toward good rather than evil. It is possible—but it is rare.

God doesn't expect you to be like Charlie Brown, constantly forgiving Lucy and believing that this time she won't pull the football away when you try to kick it. Good ol' Charlie Brown needed to say, "Lucy, I forgive you for all the times you've tricked me, but it's not going to happen again."

Nobody's perfect. Everyone gets off track from time to time. People are late when they don't mean to be. They forget to do things they promised they would do. They say things they don't mean, and immediately realize it. These are easy to forgive—and we should forgive instantly and move on.

Ruth and I have learned some important principles concerning forgiveness.

When You're Wrong, Admit It and Apologize

Have you ever been in the middle of an argument and suddenly realized that you were wrong? It's happened to me, more than once. If so, what did you do? Did you keep arguing, just to save face, or did you admit, "All of a sudden I can see that you're right"? It's the right thing to do, and it's not really as hard as you might think.

Picture this: The husband arrives home from work after a long, hard day. As soon as he walks through the door, his wife tells him that the washing machine is on the fritz.

He explodes, "Do you have to hit me with that the minute I get home? Give me a few seconds to relax, will you?"

"Wow!" she says. "You're in a bad mood tonight."

"I'm not in a bad mood," the husband insists, showing by the tone of his voice that he's in a very bad mood. "I just don't know why you always hit me with everything the minute I walk through the door!"

"Always?" she asks.

"That's right, always!"

"I was only making a comment," she protests. "I didn't mean to hit you with anything."

"Is dinner ready?" he demands, changing the subject and escalating the conflict at the same time.

Sound familiar? If not, congratulations! Most of the big fights that occur in a marriage are over silly situations like this one. It could have been nipped in the bud if the husband had caught himself right away:

> The psalmist wrote, "He has removed our sins as far from us as the east is from the west."

"You know, you're right. I *am* in a bad mood. I had a rotten day, but I didn't mean to take it out on you. I'm sorry. Please forgive me."

The three most powerful words in the English language are "I love you." The next two are "I'm sorry." Then again, neither are worth very much if there's no feeling behind them.

Accept the Apology When It's Offered—Then Forget About It

For an apology to be effective, it has to be accepted. If you want your marriage to be the best it can possibly be, you must be always willing to ask forgiveness and to give forgiveness.

Put yourself in the wife's place in the above illustration. Would you accept your husband's apology and do your best to forget about the initial exchange? Or would your husband's harsh outburst put you in a bad mood that would last for the rest of the evening—and maybe even longer? Remember those potatoes we talked about earlier? Too many people have a stash of grudges—like rotten potatoes —hidden in a personal closet somewhere. Each time our spouse does something we don't like, we pull out all those smelly spuds and start counting them. "Last week you said this, and the week before you said that . . ." It does absolutely no good to recount old hurts. It shows that you really haven't forgiven after all.

Our example is Christ, who prayed as he was being tortured and murdered, "Father, forgive them, for they don't know what they are doing" (Luke 23:34).

When God forgives, he forgets. The psalmist wrote, "He has removed our sins as far from us as the east is from the west" (Psalm 103:12).

Brennan Manning tells this wonderful story in his book *The Ragamuffin Gospel:*

Four years ago in a large city in the far West, rumors spread that a certain Catholic woman was having visions of Jesus. The reports reached the archbishop. He decided to check her out. There is always a fine line between the authentic mystic and the lunatic fringe.

"Is it true, ma'am, that you have visions of Jesus?" asked the cleric.

"Yes," the woman replied simply.

"Well, the next time you have a vision, I want you to ask Jesus to tell you the sins that I confessed in my last confession."

The woman was stunned. "Did I hear you right, bishop? You actually want me to ask Jesus to tell me the sins of your past?"

"Exactly. Please call me if anything happens."

Ten days later the woman notified her spiritual leader of a recent apparition. "Please come," she said.

Within the hour the archbishop arrived. He trusted eye-to-eye contact. "You just told me on the telephone that you actually had a vision of Jesus. Did you do what I asked?"

"Yes, bishop, I asked Jesus to tell me the sins you confessed in your last confession."

The bishop leaned forward with anticipation. His eyes narrowed.

"What did Jesus say?"

She took his hand and gazed deep into his eyes. "Bishop," she said, "these are his exact words: 'I CAN'T REMEMBER.'"[5]

Enough said.

Let me ask you a nosy question: What grudges are you carrying around with you? What are you angry about? What is it that you can't let go of and forgive?

I urge you to take a few moments right now to write up a list of all the grudges and hurts you need to get free from.

I am not suggesting that you should go back and dredge up everything your spouse has ever done to hurt you. If you've forgiven and forgotten, leave it alone. I'm talking about the things that keep resurfacing because you've never really been able to let them go. You try to forgive, but they keep coming back to you. Do you find yourself bringing up the same old hurts nearly every time you and your spouse have a disagreement? If so, put those things on your list.

> You will be lighter and freer after letting go of the grudges that have weighed you down for so long.

Once your list is completed, spend some time with God, sharing it with him and asking him to help you really forgive and forget, just as he does. Don't put the list in a drawer, where you can get it out and read it from time to time. Instead, burn or bury your list as a symbolic gesture.

Another idea is to fill a bucket with pebbles, each of which represents one action you need to forget and forgive. Then take that bucket somewhere and dump the pebbles out—preferably into a stream, pond, or other body of water— and let them carry your anger and unforgiveness away with them. You'll notice immediately how much lighter that bucket is without all of those pebbles in it.

In the same way, you will be lighter and freer after letting go of the grudges that have weighed you down for so long.

RUTH SAYS

I can remember vividly an incident when one of our children lied to us about something pretty serious. Even after several discussions about the issue, she refused to confess and apologize.

We knew she was guilty and gave her the factual evidence. Still she refused to apologize and admit her wrongdoing. Pat and I forgive our children quickly and easily when we see a truly repentant spirit. But she would not take responsibility, and even began to turn the situation around to make it look as if we, not she, somehow contributed to her plight.

I went to bed that night heartsick, with every muscle in my body aching. She knew we loved her; we told her that. But she refused to admit what she had done and, thus, we could not forgive her. We wanted to forgive, but she would not allow it—she wouldn't give us the opportunity.

Sometimes people are stubborn beyond measure. Being right is more important than anything else. For me, the emotional pain of disappointment manifested itself in a deep, aching pain in my muscles and bones. It had never happened to me before.

Notes I took from an article by Dr. Frederic Luskin of Stanford University validate what happened to me with regard to the importance of forgiveness: "Holding grudges doesn't just mess with your mood, it can lead to headaches, neck pain and stomach problems. When someone hurts you and you obsess about it, your body suffers." He added, "Can't bring yourself to turn the other cheek? Think of it this way: forgiveness is for

> your own well-being, to reduce your suffering."[6] And I might add, it can also reduce the suffering of others who want to forgive.

Don't Compare Your Spouse with Others

What does this have to do with forgiveness? Plenty. If you compare your spouse to others, it creates an atmosphere of resentment in which "yielded living" is nearly impossible.

Besides, you don't know what goes on behind closed doors. A marriage that looks like Heaven to you may be far from it when you get closer to it. Certainly it's OK to learn from other people and apply the lessons you learn to yourself. But it's not all right to tell your spouse, "Why can't you be more like so-and-so? She's so supportive of her husband. She never puts him down or snaps at me like you do to me."

> Does this sound idealistic? It's not. It can be done. Ruth and I have been living it out for the fifteen years since our relationship began.

Instead, when you see your spouse is above the fray, thank him.

"Honey, I ran into Beverly and her husband today, and he was so critical of her during our conversation. Thank you for not doing that to me."

You've given him a compliment, a blessing; and the next time he may be tempted to criticize, you can be sure he will think twice about it.

Don't compare your spouse. He or she is a unique creation of God.

Be Aggressive in Your Forgiveness

In Romans 5:20, *The Message* defines God's grace as "aggressive forgiveness." I love that, and it's true. God sent his Son to bring us forgiveness before we were even aware we'd done anything wrong. Earlier in that same chapter, Paul said, "God demonstrates his own love for us in this: While we were still sinners, Christ died for us" (Romans 5:8, *NIV*).

We can't have the attitude that says, "I'll forgive her when she asks me, but until then I'm going to be mad about it." Do you remember the Parable of the Prodigal Son? When the wayward son came home, his father ran out to meet him, embraced him, and kissed him (Luke 15:20). The young man hadn't even asked for forgiveness at this point, but his father gave it to him.

In the BEST marriages, husbands and wives expect the best from each other. They don't get their feelings hurt easily. They give each other the benefit of the doubt. Even when they have to confront each other, they try to do it in a loving spirit. They forgive gladly!

How does this translate into practical terms? If your spouse does something that hurts you, you don't jump to the conclusion that it was intentional. Nor do you let it fester. Rather, you confront it right away, in love.

The situation ought to play out like this:

"You probably don't realize this, but what you just said (or did) hurt my feelings. It sounded to me like . . ."

"Oh, I'm glad you told me. That's not at all what I meant. What I should have said was . . ."

Does this sound idealistic? It's not. It can be done. Ruth and I have been living it out for the fifteen years since our relationship began.

Seek God's forgiveness together in prayer. Pray together for forgiveness on behalf of your marriage. I suggest that you and your spouse pray out loud together, and follow this pattern:

- Praise and thank God for giving your spouse to you.
- Affirm your spouse for the qualities you most admire.
- Ask God's forgiveness for specific ways in which you have hurt your spouse.
- Ask God to help you love your spouse the way he wants you to.
- Ask God to help you fulfill your responsibilities to your spouse and your marriage.

In parts 1 and 2, we've talked about blessing and edifying your partner. I hope you've been able to implement some positive change along the way. Next up: sharing.

Reflect  & Discuss

1. Which is harder for you, to forgive or to ask for forgiveness? Explain your answer.

2. Jesus taught that we must be willing to forgive over and over again (see Matthew 18:21, 22). Has there ever been a time when you really struggled to forgive someone? Explain your answer.

3. Has there ever been a time when you struggled to ask for forgiveness? What happened?

4. It has been said that it's often easier to forgive our enemies than it is to forgive people we love. Do you think this is true? Why or why not?

5. Are there specific areas in your relationship with your spouse where you need to forgive? If so, what are they? Would asking God to help you forgive be a first step?

6. Are there specific areas where you need to ask for forgiveness? If so, what are they? Will you ask God to help you apologize?

7. Read Romans 5:20 in several versions of the Bible. How can you incorporate "God's wonderful grace" (his "aggressive forgiveness") into your marriage?

Part 3: Learning to Share

Mr. Husband,
Tear Down That Wall!

*LOVE IS MORE THAN A NOUN—IT IS A VERB; IT IS MORE THAN
A FEELING—IT IS CARING, SHARING, HELPING, SACRIFICING.*
—WILLIAM ARTHUR WARD

Not long ago, a friend of ours told us, "I feel like I'm losing my mind." She then related that she and her husband, Carl, were having communication problems.

"On Tuesday night after dinner, I noticed that Carl was very quiet. I asked him what was wrong. He said that nothing was wrong. Then he began yelling at the kids, for no reason. I again asked him what was wrong. He said that everything was all right. At bedtime I tried to get him to open up. He said that he was OK and then rolled over and went to sleep."

Tears glistened in her eyes. "I know something's wrong, but he denies it. He's been acting this way for more than a month, and I don't know what to do."

What's going on with Carl? We don't know for certain, but we hope he comes to his senses and begins treating his wife like the partner she is meant to be.

No man can build a happy marriage by erecting a wall around himself and cutting

> "I know something's wrong, but he denies it. He's been acting this way for more than a month, and I don't know what to do."

his wife out of his life. And yet, most men basically seem to be strangers to their wives. So many American men believe that a *real* man doesn't show his feelings. Often, their upbringing has reinforced the idea that men should be unemotional, undemonstrative, and unloving.

Poppycock.

You couldn't find a more manly man than Jesus Christ, nor could you find a more gentle, loving, and deeply emotional man. John 11:35 is the shortest verse in the Bible, but it is also one of the most deeply moving: "Jesus wept."

In this third section of the book, Ruth and I are going to discuss some of the lessons we've learned about sharing. We've already talked a little bit about how important it is for a husband to share himself with his wife, and for the wife to share herself with her husband. This is where it begins. But to go on and build a good marriage, husbands and wives must share other things:

- their work
- their tears and their laughter
- their hopes and dreams
- their faith

The Trouble with Romance

A friend of ours—a sweet, pretty, intelligent woman in her early forties—just got married for the fourth time. I'm keeping my fingers crossed that the fourth time is the charm, but I'm not counting on it.

There are several reasons why none of her previous three marriages has lasted more than five years. Most of all, it's because she's "in love with love." She's like a little girl who wants to be Snow White and live in bliss forever with Prince Charming. She can't get enough romance—but real love is not just romance.

> Real love is hard work. It takes a commitment to persevere when things get tough.

In fact, when I see the unhappy, disillusioned married couples all around me, I sometimes wish the whole concept of romance didn't get the press it does. There should certainly be some romance. Women need it. But real love is hard work. It takes a commitment to persevere when things get tough. It is changing dirty diapers and mopping up the vomit when one of the kids has the flu. Love is sitting down together to figure out how to get by when you don't have enough money to get to the end of the month. Love is doctor visits, PTA meetings, and going to see the principal together when Johnny acts up in school. It is discussing major purchases and making major decisions—together. It is living the day-to-day in harmony with your partner.

Unhappily married women often say, "I don't know what happened to my husband. He's changed. He's just not the same person I married." Yet in many instances, the husband hasn't changed at all. He has merely reverted back to the person he's always been. Men (and women) often act differently when they're pursuing a mate.

They do this, first of all, because they are in the throes of romantic love, and they really do believe this euphoric state has changed them forever. Romance also often blinds us to the faults of our beloved.

The second reason a man changes when he's courting a woman is that he's afraid she wouldn't want him if she knew how he really was.

I don't think a man purposely thinks, *As soon as I've got her, I'll go back to my old ways.* His intention is to become this new, better, attentive person he wants to be. But it's not that easy to change.

Some Words for the Not-Yet-Married
Get to Know Your Partner

Here's some advice for anyone contemplating marriage: get to know him (or her) before you say "I do." I learned this lesson the hard way. My first wife and I had known each other a total of eleven months before we were married, and because I was working so hard, we really didn't spend much time together. Otherwise, we would have found that we had very little in common. We tried our best, but our marriage was difficult from the beginning. It was like living in the shadow of a volcano, never knowing when the eruption was going to occur.

After we were divorced, my sister told me that based on what she saw at our wedding, she felt that our marriage was never going to last.

I was tempted to say, "I wish you'd told me then." But in her defense, it was a little late since it was our wedding day, and because love can be so blind, I probably wouldn't have been very receptive.

If you're about to get married, ask yourself how well you know your intended. What are her friends like? (Or his? Everything here pertains to women also.) What does your family think of her? Have you been through a crisis together? What is she like when things aren't going her way?

RUTH SAYS

Make sure you get your family's input. They know you really well and have some instincts that you might not have. I'll never forget the time, when I was single, I brought a male friend home to meet my parents. After dinner the first night, my father brought me into my parents' bedroom, shut the door, and said, "Baby, this man is not for you."

I knew that in my heart, but until I heard my daddy say it with love, I had denied it. He was right and I'm so glad I listened. I would have missed the great love of my life in Pat.

It's also important to get to know your beloved's friends and family. One of our daughters had been dating a young man for almost a year, and the relationship was about to get serious. But one day she said, "I love everything about John—except his friends. I don't think they're really good for him. I don't like to hang out with them, and they seem to take advantage of him because he makes more money than they do." Immediately, several red flags came into view.

John's friends were taking part in activities that she didn't like. And when she said something to him, he just waved it off as boys being boys. In your late twenties and early thirties, you are no longer a boy. So if your boyfriend or girlfriend has close friends who do things you don't like, you need to reconsider the relationship.

John had known these young men since childhood and felt a loyalty to them, no matter what they did. He most likely would have continued to let them take advantage of him, and their behavior would have created a negative impact on any serious relationship or marriage. What I told my daughter then is what I say to you: find someone whose friends encourage each other and challenge each other, someone who has friends who would never take advantage or do things that would cast shadows on the life of your beloved.

It's also important to find out about his or her family. When you walk down the aisle, you not only marry your sweet love, but also his or her family—and they may not be as sweet. Pat and I have talked to several couples who decided not to get married because they genuinely disliked the other's family and knew it would never work. Some people have gotten married anyway, despite their misgivings about each other's families. In most

> My father brought me into my parents' bedroom, shut the door, and said, "Baby, this man is not for you." I knew that in my heart, but until I heard my daddy say it with love, I had denied it.

of these cases, the situation got even worse after the wedding, and caused many problems throughout the marriage. Get to know the family really well; your life will be greatly impacted by that relationship—and you want it to be good.

If he or she already has kids, make sure you *like* them. You may grow to love them over time, but you have to like them first. And if they don't like you, walk away. It will never work.

I was fortunate in this regard. When Pat and I started dating, he suggested that I spend time with the children without him. He gave the nanny the weekend off and brought me in as a substitute nanny. It turned out to be a wonderful weekend; I had great fun with the kids and they really enjoyed me. They liked me and they told their dad how they felt. In fact, it was Karyn, Pat's oldest daughter, who later said to him, "Dad, you need to marry Ruth. She's awesome! We want her as our mother."

In our wedding vows, I took some thoughts from the book of Ruth in the Bible. After promising to love, honor, and obey Pat, I also added, "And your children shall be my children." And they have been ever since.

Imagine the Future

Work hard at keeping your physical relationship pure, not only because this is what God asks you to do, but because a hot and heavy physical relationship can blind you to some more important realities—such as, how much fun will it be to live with this person ten years from now?

> Will you still enjoy being together 18,000 dinners from now? Will you still have things to say to each other? You know, with some people, one dinner is enough.

Whenever I talk to young people who are contemplating marriage, I ask them this very important question: "Can you imagine looking across the dinner table at this person 18,000 times?"

The brows furrow. What on earth am I talking about?

"Well," I explain, "if you're married for fifty years, times 365 days each year—that comes to about 18,000 dinners, the way I figure it."

The eyes grow wider at the thought of it.

"Will you still enjoy being together 18,000 dinners from now? Will you still have things to say to each other? You know, with some people, one dinner is enough."

It's something to think about, isn't it?

Ruth and I love to people-watch when we go out anywhere, but especially at dinner. It is amazing to see married couples eat an entire dinner without saying anything to each other—*nothing!* It's like watching two robots. It is so sad to see two people who apparently have nothing to say to each other after years of marriage.

Now that the children no longer live in our house, one of the things Ruth and I enjoy the most is having dinner together. It's something pleasant to look forward to all day. I really don't want Ruth to have to cook, so we go out. Sometimes we go to Paco's (a little Mexican place we love), Olive Garden, P.F. Chang's, Cracker Barrel, or Boston Market. We vary the locations as much as we can. But the main thing is for us to get out of the house, have a nice quiet dinner, and really focus on each other.

We talk about our days, books we've read or ones we're writing, news issues, and so forth. It's a time for us to just be together and talk things through. Often we brainstorm ideas, discuss children's issues, laugh at our grandchildren's antics—anything and everything. It keeps our relationship interesting and alive. I highly recommend it.

Choose Wisely

A good employer hires very slowly. He takes his time to evaluate all the applicants and makes sure he's got the best person for the job. Choosing the person you marry is the biggest decision you'll ever make. Please choose carefully.

Bill Russell, former Boston Celtic great and longtime friend, has written a book about his relationship with his coach, Red Auerbach, called *Red and Me.*[1] In his book Bill talks about a saying a friend of his has about marriage: "Women marry men hoping to change them. Men marry women hoping they will never change."

So when Bill greets his married acquaintances, male and female, he asks, "Is the makeover finished yet?"

I'm sure that gets a laugh, but it's really serious. You can't change people. I've told my children over and over again about possible mates, "What you see is what you get. And if you don't like something now, it will only magnify itself after marriage, so make sure you really like them as well as love them."

Bill says it very well: "If you can allow yourself to accept and enjoy someone for who they are, without trying to control or change them, you can establish a lasting relationship." The person you choose to spend the rest of your life with needs to be the person you want, not the person you want to make over. So know your partner well—really well—before the walk down the aisle.

Yes, there are times when people fall in love "at first sight" and remain in love for fifty years or more, but those times are the exception, not the rule.

Not long ago, I had dinner with legendary UCLA basketball coach John Wooden. Wooden, who won an incredible ten national championships at UCLA, is ninety-nine years old and as sharp as ever. I asked him, "Coach, what would you say was the key to all your success at UCLA?"

Wooden, ever a humble and gracious man, smiled and said, "The key to our success was talent, talent, talent."

He wasn't talking about marriage, but it applies. You want to make sure you have the best possible person on your team. To sum it all up in as few words as possible:

Men, choose carefully.
Women, don't settle.

RUTH SAYS

Please, please, *please* don't settle. I've told my girls that over and over. When most women (or men, for that matter) begin to think about marriage, they often take a sheet of paper and write down all the characteristics they want in a man. He needs to be tall, dark, and handsome. He must have a good job, love children, and on and on. Don't do that. Big mistake.

Instead, think about the kind of wife you'd like to be. It's a whole different slant. The day that I first met Pat while speaking to the Orlando Magic executive team, living your values was one of the main topics. I have a way of diagramming values and roles that I use with clients, so I drew this on a flip chart on the stage. One of the values I wrote down was "wife"—I value being a good wife. Of course, I was not married at the time, and it was a great way to advertise that fact! I would tell my audiences, "Write down what you want, even if you're not there yet. And write it in the present tense."

So I wrote: "I am a wonderful wife." Pat came up to me after the workshop and asked, "Would you really make a good wife?"

The point I want every woman to understand is this: Look at how you want to be as a wife—and then find a man who will support you in that and complement it. Find someone who will allow you to be you.

"Yes," I said. And the rest, you know, is history.

The point I want every woman to understand is this: Look at how you want to be as a wife—and then find a man who will support you in that and complement it. Find someone who will allow you to be you.

Our daughter Karyn lives in Nashville now, trying to make it as a country music singer. In the process she has discovered that she has a real gift for songwriting. After hearing me say over and over, "Find the man who will let you be you, who will let you be the kind of woman and wife you want to be," she wrote the words to a song called "Woman You Wanna Be." As you read the words, think about the message.

Is he the man who makes you the woman you wanna be
Does he take your every dream and give you wings
Or does he only try to hold you down
'Cause his feet have never left the ground
Is he the man who makes you the woman you wanna be?

Is he the love of your life that you've been waiting for
Is he the one you can't live without anymore
Or is he just another dead-end road
Leading you so far from home
Is he the man who makes you the woman you wanna be?

Search your heart
Search your soul
Deep inside, you'll know

Is he the hand that shelters you when the world is cold
Is he the strength that will carry you as you grow old
Or is he one more promise bound to break
One more empty bad mistake
Is he the man who makes you the woman you wanna be?

Search your heart
Search your soul
Deep inside, you'll know
If he's the man who makes you the woman you wanna be.[2]

She got it! And she said it better than I ever did. As you look at a possible mate, think, *Is he going to encourage me and support me in my dreams? Will he be there for me through thick and thin? when we're old? after children? in hard times and good times?*

These qualities are better than tall, dark, and handsome any day. Of course, it's a nice bonus if he's good-looking, but his looks won't support you, encourage you, hold you when you cry, help you when you need it, or talk until two in the morning if you can't sleep—but his heart will.

So, ladies, find "the man who makes you the woman you wanna be," and you'll live happily ever after.

Strong Words from the Bible

The prophet Malachi had stern words for those who treat their wives poorly: "You cry out, 'Why doesn't the LORD accept my worship?' I'll tell you why! Because the LORD witnessed the vows you and your wife made when you were young. But you have been unfaithful to her, though she remained your faithful partner, the wife of your marriage vows. . . .

'I hate divorce!' says the LORD, the God of Israel. 'To divorce your wife is to overwhelm her with cruelty,' says the LORD of Heaven's Armies. 'So guard your heart; do not be unfaithful to your wife'" (Malachi 2:14, 16).

> If you don't treat your spouse well, God is going to be unhappy with you!

There are many reasons why a man should be good to his wife. But I think the above verses give the best of them all. If you don't treat your spouse well, God is going to be unhappy with you!

Think about some of the things you did for your wife before you were married that you don't do now. Did you . . .

- open the car door for her?
- pull out her chair at the dinner table?
- hold her hand whenever you could?
- listen intently to everything she had to say?
- tell her you love her?
- compliment her on her appearance?
- try to make her laugh?

Chances are you did all of those things and more. Do you do them now? If not, why not? It doesn't take much effort to do any of the above—but oh, what a difference they can make in your marriage.

RUTH SAYS

At a recent time-management workshop that I taught, I met a gentleman by the name of Andy, who sat in the front row. We had been talking about scheduling time for your priorities, especially the people in your life who are really important to you. Andy came up during a break to show me his BlackBerry task list.

I was delighted to see that his list included: "Did you tell Joann 'I love you' today?" and "Did you tell Joann how beautiful she is today?" Both of those items appeared on his list every day, with no end date, which means he never plans to stop doing them.

Andy explained to me that he and Joann had been dating for a little over two years and planned to get married at the end of the year. He said, "Some people have told me it's extremely romantic—which is how I see it. Others tell me they'd be insulted that a partner would have to remind himself to do this. All I know is, it works for us."

He went on to explain that, as a human resources manager, his workdays could be long, chaotic, and stressful—and that his fiancée understood this and was extremely patient and supportive. "It's not that we don't say 'I love you' every day, because we do," he explained. "But the BlackBerry task prompts me to actually stop what I'm doing at some point each day to let her know just how much she means to me."

Andy told me that both he and Joann were in emotionally abusive marriages before they found each other. "I know how important it is to her that she feels loved and protected, because we often talk about it. I promised her I would do both of those things. The task in my BlackBerry reminds me every day of the promise I made to her."

Little things like that can make a major difference. I'd say Andy and Joann have a recipe for success, wouldn't you?

Here's a good exercise for husbands and wives: Take a few moments right now to make a list of the things you used to do that you don't do now. Then ask yourself why you stopped doing them. Did you just get lazy? Feel unappreciated? Get so busy with life that you forgot how much those "little things" can mean? Or is there something else going on in your life that you need to deal with? Is there a wall to tear down?

Then draw up another list of things your spouse used to do that you wish he or she would still do. But don't be mean about it. And don't be unreasonable. If you do this in a loving, constructive way, it can be extremely beneficial.

> Women tend to fall in love with men who meet their need for sharing, conversation, and intimacy. They tend to *stay* in love with men who continue to meet those needs.

It won't do you any good to confront your spouse with a list of grievances and demand to be treated better. Remember that you attract more flies with honey than you do with vinegar. This can be a mutually profitable exercise if you approach it with the attitude, "Here are some of the things we used to do for each other that we don't do now. I miss them, and would like to see us get back to the way we used to be."

According to Willard F. Harley, author of the multimillion seller *His Needs, Her Needs,* women file for divorce twice as often as men. He says, "The most common reason women give for leaving their husbands is 'mental cruelty.' When legal grounds for divorce are stated, about half report they have been emotionally abused. But the mental cruelty they describe is rarely the result of their husbands' efforts to drive them crazy. It is usually husbands being indifferent, failing to communicate and demonstrating other forms of neglect."[3]

I wish I could get every husband to understand this: Women tend to fall in love with men who meet their need for sharing, conversation, and intimacy. They tend to *stay* in love with men who continue to meet those needs.

Harley writes that every husband should spend at least fifteen hours every week giving his wife his undivided attention: "Many men look at me as if they think I'm losing my mind, or they just laugh and say, 'In other words, I need a thirty-six hour day.' I don't bat an eye, but simply ask them how much time they spent giving their wives undivided attention during their courting days. Any bachelor who fails to devote something close to fifteen hours a week to his girl friend faces the strong likelihood of losing her."[4]

But what do you find to talk about during those fifteen hours? We've got a few suggestions.

Some Conversation Dos and Don'ts

Do Find Areas of Common Interest

What are you and your spouse both interested in? What was it that attracted you to each other in the first place? (Besides chemistry, I mean.) Do you share the same faith? Do you both love art or music? Did you enjoy tennis, bowling, or Scrabble before you got too busy? Have you lost interest in each other because of the demands of daily life?

Some couples make the mistake of focusing too much on their children.

Here's some advice from one of the great minds of our time, Ann Landers: "Give the needs of your mate priority. One parent put it this way: 'A husband and wife are apt to be successful parents when they put their marriage first. Don't worry about the children getting second best. Child-centered households produce neither happy marriages nor happy children.'"[5]

Do Take Interest in Your Spouse's Interests

If you discover that you and your spouse don't have that many common interests, my advice is to get some more interests. If your spouse is interested in bird-watching, you get interested in bird-watching. If she enjoys a healthy walk around the neighborhood at night, go with her.

> It's not going to kill you to see a chick flick now and then. Even if you don't care much for the movie, there's always the hand-holding and the popcorn.

It's not going to kill you to see a chick flick now and then. Even if you don't care much for the movie, there's always the hand-holding and the popcorn. The same thing goes for the woman who doesn't care about sports, but who is married to a sports nut. Even if you don't like baseball, there's nothing like the taste of a hot dog at the old ballpark. And it's a great place to people-watch!

What else is your spouse interested in? Books? Music? Current events? Theater? Not only will you improve your relationship with your spouse by learning to take an interest in such things, you just might expand your own horizons as well.

Bear in mind, I'm not saying that the husband and wife should do *everything* together. Both of you need some time that's set aside for you, and you alone. Plus, having unique interests adds some mystery and spice to a relationship. There must be a proper balance between togetherness and space.

Don't Monopolize the Conversation

Conversation is supposed to be a two-way street. It's not a monologue. You've got to give your spouse a chance to talk. If you

> I find that one major difference in the way men and women converse is that women tell a story and men give a news report.

interrupt every time she opens her mouth, she might stop trying. If you go on and on and on, she might stop listening altogether.

Although there are exceptions, I find that one major difference in the way men and women converse is that women tell a story and men give a news report. In other words, women build up to the big ending, while men give the headline up front and then fill in all the details.

Either way of communicating can be fine, and either can be exasperating.

People who talk in stories sometimes give way too much detail. You might lose your spouse's attention if you wander all over the place, or if you spend too much time trying to make sure you get all the facts straight. I have an acquaintance who talks to me like this: "Pat, did you hear about what happened to me last Wednesday? Well, I was on my way to the grocery store when . . . no, wait. I think it was Tuesday. Or was it Wednesday? Hmmm? Well, anyway, I was on my way to . . . wait, it was Tuesday for sure. And I'd already been to the grocery store, so I must have been heading to the dry cleaners . . ."

Do you know anybody like that? I really do like this person, but I admit that I sometimes try to avoid him. I just don't have half an hour to hear a story that could take less than five minutes to tell! Some details are not that important, so leave them out.

On the other extreme is the person who talks in headlines, often leaving his spouse wanting more:

"I heard that Jerry's taking a job in Denver and they'll be moving soon."

"What? How soon will they be leaving?"

"Uh . . . I'm not really sure."

"Well, what kind of job is it?"

"I don't know. I didn't ask him."

"And what about our small group? Are they going to find someone else to lead it?"

"Good question. I should have asked about that."

The storyteller and the headline guy need to learn how to meet somewhere in the middle.

> It is flat-out disrespectful to read the paper, watch television, fill out paperwork, or do any such thing while your spouse is talking to you.

Don't Correct Your Spouse

While your spouse is telling others about something that happened, don't butt in. I know it can be maddening when he or she is getting the facts all mixed up. Most of us have a strong urge to correct.

I was in a restaurant not long ago and overheard the gentleman at the next table telling his wife about something he'd seen in the newspaper. I'd read the same story, and this guy had everything terribly twisted and confused. I felt like interrupting and explaining what had really happened; however, it wasn't important, and it was certainly none of my business.

So what if your spouse gets a few details mixed up? You wouldn't want to ignore an out-and-out lie, but otherwise, stay out of it. Correcting each other, and thus embarrassing each other, in front of other people is most definitely not good for your relationship.

Do Give Your Spouse Your Undivided Attention

We live in an age of multitasking. When I'm stuck in traffic, I'm always amazed to see what other drivers are trying to do. I often see women trying to put on their makeup while they drive. I've seen people reading books propped up against the steering wheel. The other day, I saw a guy shaving with an electric razor. And even though it's now illegal in several states, thousands of drivers are texting or talking on their cell phones.

I worry about people who do such things. They apparently don't understand that a moment's inattention can be deadly. Driving is one of those areas where multitasking is definitely *not* a good thing. Driving a car demands your full attention.

So does talking to your spouse. It is flat-out disrespectful to read the paper, watch television, fill out paperwork, or do any such thing while your spouse is talking to you. It gives the impression that you're thinking, *What you're saying is so insignificant, I can listen with only half my brain.* Or, *Listening to you is a waste of my time. That's why I have to find something else to do while you're talking.*

So don't do it. If something urgent is going on and you really don't have time to talk right now, say so. "Honey, I really want to hear what you have to say, but I have to get this report done. Can you give me fifteen minutes, and then we'll sit down and talk about it?"

Do Go Beyond the Superficial

"I can't talk to my husband about anything. He turns everything I say into a joke. He doesn't take me seriously, and he refuses to confront things that have to be confronted."

"My wife and I never have a pleasant conversation. She always has a long list of issues we need to talk about. I always feel exhausted and overwhelmed after about fifteen minutes."

Do either of the above comments sound familiar? This couple needs to meet in the middle. He must understand that there are serious issues that have to be talked about, confronted, and dealt with. She ought to lighten up and realize that it's OK to have some fun once in a while. Both partners have to give a little bit.

Remember that a successful marriage is one in which both partners are willing to give 100 percent. If your marriage is in trouble, it may not need to be worked on, but rather, *participated in,* shared. If you see that you and your spouse need to improve your communication skills, I urge you to follow these Ten Commandments of Good Communication:

I. Work at it.

II. Learn to compromise with your spouse.

III. Be open and seek to understand what your partner is saying.

IV. Affirm your spouse by showing that you are interested in what he or she has to say.

V. Be positive and encouraging.

VI. Share from the heart.

VII. Don't try to read your spouse's mind. Don't read into things that he or she says.

VIII. Be honest at all times.

IX. Respond to what your spouse has to say.

X. Timing is important. If you have something deep or difficult to say, look for the right time to say it.

Real sharing can happen when you recognize—and tear down!—any walls that are in the way. When both people in the marriage are committed to making it work, it's amazing how God can craft your unique combination of strengths into a satisfying marriage. You don't need a new partner! You may only need a new attitude.

You wouldn't trade in your car simply because it needed a minor tune-up. And yet, some people walk away from a marriage when a few minor adjustments could have saved it. Please examine yourself and see if there are areas in which you need to work on being more loving and attentive in the way you relate to your spouse. Don't put it off. Your marriage is much too important.

Reflect & Discuss

1. How much time do you and your spouse spend together each week? Is it anywhere near fifteen hours? Do you feel that this is sufficient? Explain.

2. What specific changes could you make in your schedules so that the two of you could have more time together?

3. What are some of the common interests you and your spouse share?

4. Does your spouse have other areas of interest you could take part in? If so, what are they?

5. Do *you* have any other areas of interest in which your spouse could be involved? If so, what are they?

6. Read Malachi 2:14-16. Is there anything you need to repent of before the Lord? Is there anything you need to ask your spouse's forgiveness for? Do it.

7. What changes, if any, do you feel you need to make in the way you communicate with your spouse?

8. Which of the dos and don'ts in this chapter are the most difficult for you? Why?

9. What action steps will you take to improve the way you share yourself with your spouse?

Share and Conquer

CARRY EACH OTHER'S BURDENS, AND IN THIS WAY YOU WILL FULFILL THE LAW OF CHRIST.

—GALATIANS 6:2, NIV

When Robert and Rachel Crawford celebrated fifty-two years together, their friends and family asked for their recipe for a successful marriage. It wasn't just that their marriage had lasted so long, but that the two of them still seemed to be so much in love.

I no longer have the source of their story, but I did keep the eight reasons they gave for fifty-two years of marital happiness:

1. Our love for Christ and each other.
2. Our commitment to each other.
3. Our common goal of serving Christ and making him known.
4. Our willingness to admit when we were wrong and ask forgiveness.
5. Our willingness to concede when the other person was right and we were wrong.
6. Never letting misunderstandings or disagreements go unsettled, without discussing them and expressing our love and confidence in each other.

7. Sharing each other's joys and sorrows.
8. Giving each other the freedom to make important decisions alone, if necessary, knowing we would have the other's support.

I love their list. The only bits of wisdom I might add come from Percy and Florence Arrowsmith of Hereford, England. In 2005, they were listed by the *Guinness World Records* as the world's longest-married couple, with eighty years of wedded bliss to their credit. The young couple, 105 and 100 years of age respectively, said the secret to their long marriage is that they still work at it. Florence said that she and her husband always go to bed as friends, and if they've had a disagreement, "We . . . always make up before we go to sleep with a kiss and a cuddle."

> Gentlemen, love your woman unconditionally. Ladies, show your man respect.

Percy had one other piece of advice. All husbands, he said, should use these words as often as possible: "Yes, dear."[1]

You already know that I'm a voracious reader, and I read just about every marriage book that comes along. If I were asked to summarize in one short statement everything the marriage experts are saying, it would be this: "Men, your wife needs to be loved. Women, your guy needs to be respected."

Which comes first—the love or the respect? I'll let you figure that out. All I know is, gentlemen, love your woman unconditionally. Ladies, show your man respect. According to marriage experts, you will have discovered the magical secret to a happy, lasting marriage. Of course, the experts got it from Scripture: "Each man must love his wife as he loves himself, and the wife must respect her husband" (Ephesians 5:33).

Walk a Mile in Each Other's Shoes

A huge lesson Ruth and I have learned during our years together is the importance of trying to see things through each other's point of view. For instance, I can't remember Ruth ever saying anything to make me feel guilty about not helping out more around the house. When I'm home, I always do everything I can to help out. But there are times when I'm rarely home. I've discovered that if the plumbing is going to back up, it's almost certainly going to do it when I'm away from home. If the air conditioner goes out, I'll probably be a thousand miles away. Yet despite the fact that Ruth is left to tend to an awful lot of messes, she never complains about it. She knows that I'm on the road because it's my job and my calling—my way of providing for the family.

We both do our best to live up to Ephesians 4:2: "Always be humble and gentle. Be patient with each other, making allowance for each other's faults because of your love." A little understanding can go a long, long way toward building a winning marriage.

My friend, does your wife know that you empathize with her and care about her when she's had a bad day? Does she know that she'll always find a listening ear when she needs to vent? Can she come to you with her biggest fears and worries, knowing that you will listen sympathetically, and that you won't put her down or make her feel she's being silly? Sometimes a woman needs her husband's reassurance that everything is going to be all right. And she needs to hear it in a loving, kind, nonjudgmental way.

> "Always be humble and gentle. Be patient with each other, making allowance for each other's faults because of your love."

To the ladies I say, when your husband's having a terrible day at work, does he look forward to coming home at the end of it all and finding refuge in your arms? Does he know that you appreciate what he goes through to provide for his family? It is terrible for a man to feel that he has no refuge at all from the storms of life. He needs to know that you love and respect him, even when his clients, bosses, or customers have been tearing him apart all day.

Please forgive me if the two examples I've just given seem a bit stereotypical. As I've said previously, I understand that most women work outside the home these days. My point is that husbands and wives need to share each other's burdens—inside and outside the home. The wife may not work for the same company that employs her husband, but she's his business partner just the same. If the wife

> Husbands and wives need to share each other's burdens—inside and outside the home.

is a full-time homemaker, that doesn't mean the husband can step aside and say, "Whatever happens here is your business." He must be his wife's partner, sharing in running a well-ordered home and family.

I don't mean to imply that when your wife is cooking, you have to be in the kitchen with her, chopping onions and handing her the utensils she needs. If your wife loves to cook, and you can't seem to boil water without burning it, then by all means stay out of her way. It's all right if there are some specific areas where you've agreed that one or the other of you is in charge. Perhaps the wife takes charge of the kitchen, while the husband makes sure the kids get their homework done. Or perhaps the wife likes to garden, so the husband lets her take care of the yard while he tends to the vacuuming and the laundry.

It doesn't really matter how you do it. It's just important that you share.

Listed below are some big and small decisions that most families face. Ideally, both partners in a marriage will work together to arrive at decisions that are agreeable to both. Is this the way it works in your family? Who decides the answers to questions like these:

- Where will we go for vacation this year?
- Is it time to buy a new car? And if so, what kind of car do we want?
- Will we send the kids to public or private school?
- Which do we need first, a new washer or a new high-definition TV?
- What movie are we going to see on Friday night?
- Whose folks will we spend the holidays with this year?
- Should we be putting more money into savings?
- Should we think about selling our house and looking for something bigger (or smaller)?
- Should we rebalance our investments?
- How often can we afford to eat out?

In some families, either the wife or the husband is a dictator who makes all the decisions. That's bad, for obvious reasons.

In other families, either the wife or the husband abdicates all responsibility to the other. Often this is done in the guise of being a nice guy, as in, "Whatever you want is fine with me. I just want you to be happy." This isn't good either because it puts way too much responsibility on the other partner. It also gives the impression that you don't really care about anything, or that you don't want to participate in a decision because you're afraid it might turn out wrong. For example, if you buy that new car and it turns out to be a lemon, you can always say, "Well, I really wanted a Toyota anyway."

Work together. Share the load. Be partners!

Not long ago, I talked to a fellow named Roger who told me how he almost ruined his life. He did it by doing something most of us have probably wanted to do at one time or another. He felt that his boss was picking on him—so he quit.

"I didn't think twice about it," he said. "I'd had it up to here, so I just said, 'You can't push me around anymore. I'm out of here!' and I walked out the door. I wish I had thought about it," he continued. "I wish I had talked it over with my wife. I wasn't thinking about her, or our daughter. I was only thinking about myself."

To be fair, he also thought it would be easy to get another job.

"I lived in a small town. I knew just about everybody. I figured somebody would hire me right away."

Instead, he was out of work for nearly a year. The stress became too much for his wife, who took their daughter and went home to live with her parents. Roger sat at home, darkly depressed, and turned to the bottle for comfort.

Today Roger is putting the pieces of his life together with the help of a Christian ministry. But that wouldn't be necessary if he had thought things through and realized that some decisions are much too important to be made alone.

Divide the Sorrow, Multiply the Joy

It's easy to have a great marriage when everything is going your way. The sun is shining. The sky is blue. The job is good. The future seems unlimited. Your partner is beautiful.

But the true test of a couple's love for each other occurs when the rain starts falling. What happens when the husband is laid off and has trouble finding another job? Or when a child is born with a mental or physical disability? Or when the wife finds a lump in her breast?

Every adult in the entire world has cried at one time or another. Tragedies happen. Tears are part and parcel of life here on earth. God knew this was going to happen, so he gave us each other to lean on. Jesus promised, "Here on earth you will have many trials and sorrows" (John 16:33), so we shouldn't be surprised when they happen.

Some people teach that Christians shouldn't suffer. They say that anyone who is "a child of the King" should basically float through life. They teach that God wants to bless us, so it's a sign of faith to drive an expensive car, live in an upscale neighborhood, and be strong and healthy until God calls you home.

Frankly, that's not the way I see it. In the Bible I read, Jesus says, "If any of you wants to be my follower, you must turn from your selfish ways, take up your cross daily, and follow me" (Luke 9:23). I believe that God wants to bless us. But I also believe it is much more important to him that we grow in faith, courage, and boldness than it is that we have all the things we want.

> Tears are part and parcel of life here on earth. God knew this was going to happen, so he gave us each other to lean on.

Yet he wants us to know that he's with us *in the storm.* In John 16:33, Jesus went on to say, "Take heart, because I have overcome the world."

Our Lord also wants us to lean on each other, and especially our life partners. The Bible says, "Among the Lord's people, women are not independent of men, and men are not independent of women. For although the first woman came from man, every other man was born from a woman, and everything comes from God" (1 Corinthians 11:11, 12). In this passage, the apostle Paul says that men and women in general, and husbands and wives in particular, must depend on and rely on one another.

In the very second chapter of the Bible, God looked down at the man he had created and said, "It is not good for the man to be alone. I will make a helper who is just right for him" (Genesis 2:18). That suitable helper, of course, was the first woman, Eve. God did not design us to be self-sufficient. He expected human beings to depend on each other, and especially in marriage.

About a year ago, a man I know was laid off at work. His story wasn't unique, especially not in these turbulent economic times. My friend had always done a good job of providing for his family. They lived in a gated community, in a huge house with a pool.

He told me he was trying hard to find another job, but there were none to be had. At first his wife was sympathetic. Sadly, that changed as the weeks went by. She wondered out loud if he was trying hard enough to find another job. She suggested that he must have done something wrong on his résumé. She began recoiling when he tried to touch her. Then she asked him to start sleeping in the guest bedroom.

> He told me he was trying hard to find another job, but there were none to be had. At first his wife was sympathetic. Sadly, that changed as the weeks went by. She wondered out loud if he was trying hard enough.

Understand that I'm not talking about the Wicked Witch of the West. This is a nice, friendly woman—a good wife and mother—who simply couldn't take the pressure. Her husband told me that she seemed to be as bewildered by her own reaction to his sudden unemployment as he was.

Fortunately, before their marriage wound up in divorce court, he found another job. Crisis over. Everything is back to normal.

This couple seems to have weathered the crisis, but I wonder about their future. Now that the hard times are behind them, neither one of them wants to talk about things. So what's going to happen when the next setback comes along—as it surely will?

I've seen couples who were brought together by tragedy, and I've seen couples who were torn apart by tragedy. In the same way, some people turn toward God when trouble comes along, and some people turn *away* from him.

I have no way of knowing anything about you or what's going on in your life. But I'm praying for you as I write these words, that no great tragedy will ever come into your life, and that all of your troubles will be small ones. And yet, anyone who lives long enough will go through times of great loss. Our parents and others we dearly love will get old and die. We'll lose aunts and uncles, older siblings and friends, teachers and preachers we've admired. Trials are bound to come, just as Jesus promised, and it's not such a bad idea to plan ahead how we're going to handle them—just as a professional athlete knows what his move should be in every situation.

Consider the Major League shortstop. He's thinking ahead on every play. He knows what he will do with the ball if it comes to him. He knows what he's going to do if the ball is hit to one of his teammates. He knows whether he should play in or back at double-play depth. He's constantly aware of how many outs there are, whether there are runners on base, and the strengths and weaknesses of the opposing hitter. It's not by sheer luck that the greatest shortstops seem to be in the right place at the right time.

> Lean *toward* each other, rather than away from each other.

What can you do to stand strong when it seems like the Big Bad Wolf is huffing and puffing and trying to blow your house down?

Refuse to Blame Your Spouse for the Problem

It wasn't my friend's fault that he got laid off. Don't ever play the blame game for any reason. Finding fault and pointing fingers is totally counterproductive. I've seen some good basketball teams fall apart after players started blaming each other for a couple of close losses. The same thing can happen to a marriage.

Strive to Have a "We" Attitude

My boss, Rich DeVos, owner of the Orlando Magic, began his company at his kitchen table in 1959. That's when he and his partner, the late Jay Van Andel, launched Amway. They partnered together for decades and built Amway into a multibillion dollar, worldwide business. One day I asked Rich how they grew the company and what he considered the key to their success. He didn't have to think about it. His answer came immediately: "We each had areas of responsibility where our strengths were greatest. But if things went wrong, we never blamed each other or second-guessed each other. We never pointed fingers and said, 'If you'd just done that' or 'What were you thinking about when you did that?'" That key principle of human relations formed the foundation of a global business.

I urge you to be the same way in your marriage. Do what you can to serve and care for each other. Lean *toward* each other, rather than away from each other. Don't expect your spouse to wave a magic wand and make things all right for you. And don't try to carry the entire load for him or her. Share each other's burdens.

Show How Much You Value Your Spouse

Let her know that you love her and are committed to your marriage. This is especially important at a time when she may feel that her whole world has fallen apart.

Let Her Deal with a Difficult Situation Her Own Way

If she needs to cry, let her cry, and don't get angry about it. Some men have a hard time dealing with their wives' tears because they've been brought up to feel that any displays of emotion are inappropriate. I have three important words of advice for these guys: deal with it. If she needs to talk it out, listen. If she needs some alone time, give it.

Pray About It

This is the most important thing, and should probably come first, before all that I have said till now. How do you stand strong when the storms of life come your way? Pray—before, during, and after.

> How do you stand strong when the storms of life come your way? Pray—before, during, and after.

The Bible promises, "Are any of you suffering hardships? You should pray. Are any of you happy? You should sing praises. Are any of you sick? You should call for the elders of the church to come and pray over you, anointing you with oil in the name of the Lord. Such a prayer offered in faith will heal the sick, and the Lord will make you well. And if you have committed any sins, you will be forgiven" (James 5:13-15).

Sounds to me like a great prescription for dealing with all of life's woes.

Have Fun Together

I believe most married couples could benefit a great deal from listening to Garrison Keillor: "If the romance or marriage needs help, the answer almost always is Have More Fun. Drop your list of grievances and go ride a roller coaster. Take a brisk walk. Dance. Take a trip to Duluth. Read Dickens."[2]

Did you have fun together when you were dating? Of course you did.

Do you have fun now? Probably. But if you're like most couples who've been married for a while, chances are you don't have as much fun now as you used to. But why not?

I understand that life is full of challenges and stresses. I saw a bumper sticker the other day that said, "If you're not upset, you obviously don't know what's going on." I'm not sure I buy that one, because if you really know what's going on, you know that God's got it all under control. Life isn't one continuous laugh riot, but that doesn't mean you can't have fun.

> God is not the landlord who's always yelling, "Turn down that music or I'll call the cops!"

Believe it or not, some people don't like it when Ruth and I talk about having fun. They say things like, "Life is serious. We weren't put on this earth to have fun."

Where did we ever get the idea that God is a killjoy who wants us to go around with a long face? He's not the landlord who's always yelling, "Turn down that music or I'll call the cops!" God wants us to enjoy the world he created for us. His laws aren't meant to keep us from having fun, but rather to ensure that we make the most of our time here—that we don't indulge in behaviors that will destroy our minds, bodies, and souls.

Look at what Jesus' critics said about him. They called him a drunkard and a glutton. They were angry that he spent time with people of questionable character. They demanded to know why he didn't fast and follow their traditions. Jesus certainly knew what it was like to feel deep sorrow. But he also knew what it was like to have fun. Furthermore, when Jesus' disciples asked him who would be greatest in the kingdom of Heaven, he drew their attention to a little child.

Perhaps it's not a coincidence that, as behavioral scientists tell us, the average child laughs 150 times every day, whereas the average adult laughs 15 times.[3] We need to rediscover childish joy. If God didn't want us to have fun, why did he give us things like rainbows, sunsets, cool breezes, or fragrant flowers?

Pete Carroll of the University of Southern California is one of the most successful college football coaches of the current era. Every year since Carroll took over in 2001, USC has been in the running for the national title, having won two championships and a school record thirty-four games in a row.

Heisman Trophy winner Reggie Bush, who went on to play for the New Orleans Saints, said of his former coach, "He makes it fun for our team. Everybody loves playing for him. That's one of the key things—it doesn't have to always be about just business. . . . Our practices are intense, . . . but they're fun at the same time."[4] You don't have to be serious all the time to be a winner in life—or marriage.

And here's another point in favor of fun: it's good for you! According to healthier-you.com:

> To check the health benefits of laughter, scientists at the University of Maryland tested the blood vessels of 20 healthy volunteers after they watched both a comedy and a drama. They found that laughing dramatically improved the working of the endothelium, the lining of the blood vessels. The blood vessels dilated better and blood flow improved 22 percent. The reverse was true of the drama. The vessels constricted and blood flow decreased 35 percent. The changes lasted 30 to 45 minutes after watching each movie segment.
>
> The researchers concluded that 15 minutes of laughter a day may go a long way toward good health.[5]

The same article reported on a study at Vanderbilt University, where researchers found that hearty laughter can burn calories equivalent to several minutes of working out on a rowing machine or exercise bike!

There are numerous studies and reports on the health benefits of fun and laughter. I really do believe that having fun can save your life—and your marriage.

By the way, the healthiest people I know are those who don't mind a hearty laugh at their own expense. It's OK to realize that you're not perfect, to admit that you're a human being who makes mistakes. If you learn to laugh at yourself, you'll win the respect of other people and lessen the stress that comes from striving so hard to meet your own expectations.

A sense of humor is a great asset—in marriage or any other area of life. There are bound to be tough times and difficult days. But you can get through them with your sense of humor and optimism for the future intact.

Give yourself and your wife a fun booster shot when needed. Look at the old photo albums and reminisce about the great times you've had. Be reminded of how important it is to spend time together doing things you both enjoy. Especially if you're a little out of sorts with each other, get out the photo album. You just can't stay mad at each other when you're looking at all those photos of the two of you with big smiles across your faces and thinking about all the fun you've had as a couple.

RUTH SAYS

Pat has satellite radio in his car and loves it, not only because he can tune in sports from all over the country but also because he can listen to oldies music. One day I'll never forget, Pat and I had gone to lunch, and he was bringing me home before going back to the office. We were holding hands, just listening to the music, tapping our feet and singing along.

> When Pat parked in the driveway, he turned the music up really loud, came around to my side of the car to open the door, took me in his arms, and began dancing me around the driveway.

When Pat parked in the driveway, he turned the music up really loud, came around to my side of the car to open the door, took me in his arms, and began dancing me around the driveway. We were laughing so hard, our housekeeper, Lauretta, came out to see where the "noise" was coming from. When she saw us, she stopped dead in her tracks and howled with laughter.

Understand that Pat has no rhythm and will never be invited to appear on *Dancing with the Stars*. Still, I'll always remember how much fun we had and how hard we laughed that day. It was a simple thing, really, but it will forever be one of my favorite memories. It's times like these that cause us to recommit to keeping a fun, joyful spirit in our relationship.

Share the Bible

I think it's very important for husbands and wives to read the Bible together. Just listen to what some of America's heroes have said about this book[6]:

- "It is impossible to rightly govern the world without God and the Bible." (George Washington)
- "I believe the Bible is the best gift God has ever given to man." (Abraham Lincoln)
- "That Book is the rock on which our Republic rests." (Andrew Jackson)
- "The secret of my success? It is simple. It is found in the Bible." (George Washington Carver)
- "It is impossible to enslave mentally or socially a Bible-reading people. The principles of the Bible are the groundwork of human freedom." (Horace Greeley)

Not only is the Bible full of wisdom about how husbands and wives should relate to each other, but it's full of practical advice that can help us live our lives to the fullest. Here are just some of the wonderful things you can learn as you read the Bible together:

- "You are precious" to God. (Isaiah 43:4)
- God has a wonderful plan for your life. (Jeremiah 29:11)
- God loves you "with an everlasting love." (Jeremiah 31:3)
- God's gift to you is eternal life through faith in Jesus Christ. (John 3:16)
- If you have accepted Christ as Lord and Savior, your sins have been forgiven completely. (Colossians 1:14)

- God will give you everything you need. (Philippians 4:19)
- God will give you wisdom if you ask for it. (James 1:5)
- God will give you help whenever you need it. (Hebrews 4:16)

Even those who don't believe in God can benefit from reading the Bible. I think of Thomas Jefferson, who pasted together his own Bible after cutting out all references to Jesus' miracles. Jefferson frequently read his Bible and was guided by the moral principles he found there, though sadly, he did not accept Christ as the divine Son of God.

For those who do have a personal relationship with God, reading the Bible is an entirely different experience. It is a living document that speaks directly to the believer's heart. Almost every time I pick up the Book, God shows me something I've never noticed before. I've had people tell me that they tried to read the Bible before they had accepted Christ, and they just couldn't get into it. Many passages seemed dry and boring. But after they turned their lives over to Christ, they found that God's Word became so exciting, they wanted to read it all the time.

> Almost every time I pick up the Book, God shows me something I've never noticed before.

I hope that you are reading God's Word through the eyes of faith. Here are some practical guidelines that have helped Ruth and me immensely:

- Set aside a regular time for reading the Bible together each day.
- Before you read together, ask God to help you understand what you are reading and how it applies to you and your marriage.
- Take some time to think about and talk about what you are reading.
- Write down at least one thing you have learned that you can incorporate into your life.
- Don't give up or be discouraged if you come across some verses that are difficult to understand. When this happens, concentrate on applying what you *do* understand—and God will reveal the rest to you in due time.
- Try reading different translations of the Bible to gain new insight.

The Bible is a love letter from God. It tells us how he expects us to live and gives us the good news that forgiveness is always available when we mess up. It's full of God's promises to his children. It lets us know that we are not alone. It promises us that life does not end at the grave and that there will one day be a happy reunion with those who've gone on before us. What's more, the Bible tells us what we need to do to get to Heaven so we can live forever with God.

> She never would have been happy with that young man, because they would not be sharing in the most important part of a relationship—faith in God.

One day as I was in a radio studio waiting to go on the air, I started talking to the young woman who produced the program that was having me on as a guest. She told me she lived in the Northeast, and when I asked how she liked it, she said it was hard because she had not been able to find a church.

When I asked about her love life, she said she had just broken up with a longtime boyfriend.

I asked her why.

"Because he doesn't like church," she responded.

"Then you did the right thing," I told her. She never would have been happy with that young man, because they would not be sharing in the most important part of a relationship—faith in God.

Ruth and I love reading the Bible to each other and to our children. It brings us closer to Christ and to each other. We also like to memorize Scriptures so we can draw strength from God's Word. When I was fifty-five years old, I ran in my first marathon in Orlando. Frankly, some of my friends thought I was crazy. When I told them what I was planning, they rolled their eyes and said, "You're going to run twenty-six miles? Yeah, right!" Well, I did it, and it was one of the most exhilarating experiences of my life. Since then, I've run in fifty-two marathons all over the country.

I don't set any speed records. Usually, the winners have showered, dressed, and gone out to dinner by the time I cross the finish line. But I have tons of fun, and it's still a thrill to know that God has given me enough strength and energy to run that far.

After my first couple of races, I realized that I have quite a bit of time on my hands when I'm running a marathon. So I decided to write some of my favorite Scripture verses on index cards and carry them with me. As I'm running, I pull out a verse and memorize it. Once I've got it down, I pull out the next one. I have a wonderful time exercising my body and my spirit, and the verses I've memorized have often come back to me at just the time I needed them.

Remember that old computer-programming acronym GIGO? It stood for "Garbage In, Garbage Out." Jesus said pretty much the same thing two thousand years ago. "A good person produces good things from the treasury of a good heart, and an evil person produces evil things from the treasury of an evil heart. What you say flows from what is in your heart" (Luke 6:45).

Fill yourself with God's Word and you can't go wrong. I hope you'll do what I've done. No, I'm not talking about running in a marathon, but rather, using whatever time you have to memorize God's Word so that it becomes second nature to you.

As you and your spouse share the Bible, I know you'll find that what the psalmist said is true: "Your word is a lamp to guide my feet and a light for my path" (Psalm 119:105).

Sharing—as we've outlined in part 3—is not just something preschoolers do. It's the vital *S* in The BEST Game Plan for a Winning Marriage. And if you will do it consistently, you'll have some fun along the way, and you may even surpass the Crawfords' fifty-two years of marital happiness!

| Reflect & Discuss |

1. Read Galatians 6:2. What are some of the burdens you need to share with your spouse? How can you share them?

2. What are some of your spouse's burdens that you need to help carry? What can you do to help ease the load?

3. How are decisions made in your family? Are you and your spouse both comfortable with this? If not, what changes are needed in your decision-making process?

4. Read James 1:5. Do you and your spouse pray for wisdom before making major decisions? If so, how has the Lord answered your prayers?

5. What ideas do you have for injecting more fun into your marriage?

6. Read Acts 17:11 and 2 Timothy 3:16, 17. Based on these two passages, do you feel that you and your spouse should spend more time reading the Bible together? What changes will you make in your daily or weekly schedule in order to accomplish this?

7. The next opportunity you and your spouse have some extended time to read the Bible, try reading all of Psalm 119. See how many descriptions of the Bible and promises of God you can find in this powerful psalm. Then commit some of the verses to memory the next time you walk, jog around the block . . . or run a marathon.

Part 4: The Power of Touch

Touching: The Icing on the Wedding Cake

WE WILDLY UNDERESTIMATE THE POWER OF THE TINIEST PERSONAL TOUCH.

—TOM PETERS

Someone is blushing.

"Are you going to talk about sex in this section of the book?"

Yes!

But not just yet.

Of course, sex is included in the category of touch, and it is an important aspect of every healthy marriage. But there's much more to touching than sex.

I believe that one of the problems in modern-day America is that people don't touch each other because they're afraid of what other people will think. I understand that it is important to respect another person's private space. And I also know that some people engage in inappropriate touching. But I still think it's sad that we've allowed ourselves to become so isolated. After all, we're social beings. We need physical contact with others, and especially with our life partners.

According to an article on the Web site thewellspring.com:

> There is a biological need for touch, an actual hunger for touch that can be met only in contact with another human being. This was first

discovered during the nineteenth century, when children who had been abandoned at birth and transferred to foundling homes died by the thousands. They literally wasted away, despite the fact that they were fed, kept clean, and protected from danger. The condition, known as *marasmus* (from the Greek, meaning 'wasting away'), claimed the lives of nearly 100 percent of the infants under the age of one in U.S. foundling hospitals as late as 1920.

The article goes on to say:

The lack of sufficient touch has far-reaching effects on our development and shows itself in problematic ways when we reach maturity. Some destructive means of compensating for the unmet need for touch may include:
- overeating—trying to fill an inner void left by unmet oral needs, and deadening the pain of emotional isolation, often through eating fatty foods . . . that . . . dampen the emotions
- self-destructive habits, such as smoking, nail-biting, pulling out hair, rubbing the skin excessively, and even self-mutilation
- compulsive sex, physical violence and aggressiveness, rape, and other forms of sexual abuse[1]

> Husbands and wives, caught up in work and family obligations, are often too exhausted to give each other the affection needed.

I believe that the lack of affectionate touching creates a serious problem for many married couples. Husbands and wives, caught up in work and family obligations, are often too exhausted to give each other the affection needed. We rarely know our neighbors or live close to parents and grandparents. We are suspicious of strangers and carefully guard our personal space when we meet new people. Only in small cities and towns in America do you find the connectedness and community needed to "keep in touch."

In Romans 16:16 Christians are encouraged to greet one another with "a holy kiss" (*NIV*). Some of the modern versions have translated this more in the sense of "give each other a handshake." It seems to me that something very warm and real has been lost over the centuries.

Sadly, our reluctance to have physical contact with other people may carry over into marriage. We're just not used to touching each other in gentle, loving ways that have nothing to do with sex. And any marriage that doesn't include whopping amounts of hugging, caressing, patting, and stroking will never be all that it could be.

A simple, loving touch can say so much. It says:

- "You are cared for."
- "You are not alone."
- "Don't be afraid."

It can ease our pain. It can make us feel safe and secure in the middle of a frightening storm.

The eighth chapter of Matthew contains one of my favorite stories from the life of Jesus. Matthew tells us that after Christ preached the Sermon on the Mount, a man with leprosy came and knelt before him. "Lord," he said, "if you are willing, you can heal me and make me clean."

Jesus responded by reaching out and touching him. "'I am willing,' he said. 'Be healed!' And instantly the leprosy disappeared" (Matthew 8:2, 3).

Why did Jesus touch the leper? He didn't have to. He could have spoken a single word and the man would have been healed.

I believe that what Jesus did was a loving act of compassion toward someone who hadn't experienced a gentle, caring touch from another human being in a long, long time—perhaps not for years. Leprosy was a devastating, humiliating illness that isolated a person and kept him apart from any one-to-one contact with another person. Nobody touched a leper. It was considered dangerous. It made one ceremonially unclean.

If you were a leper, you probably lived in a camp on the outskirts of the city, surviving on scraps of food other people threw out. If you went on a journey, you had to yell out, "Unclean! Unclean!" as you walked along, so "normal" people would not be contaminated by getting too close to you. You couldn't hold a job. You couldn't ever hug or hold anyone you loved—your spouse, your parents, your children, or your best friend.

Can you imagine what it was like to live like that? And can you imagine the emotions that leper felt as Jesus reached out and, with a loving hand, set him free from the pain of isolation, rejection, and disease?

I love what Amy Nappa says in her book, *A Woman's Touch:* "When Jesus walked the earth, people everywhere wanted to touch him and be touched by him. Through his touch, the blind could see and the lame could walk. The sick were healed. And people caught in the snare of sin were set free. No wonder the crowds clamored for the touch of the Savior!"

Then she asks some questions all married people should consider: "Do people long for your touch—or do you sense that they draw back? Is your touch as valuable as gold to your loved ones, as sweet as chocolate? Or is it as hard as nails? Does your touch bring blessing and healing to the people around you, or pain and heartache?"[2]

A Tragic Lesson

Do you remember the shocking news that came out of Romania after the fall of the Communist government there in 1989? As many as 10,000 children were discovered living in austere, warehouse-like state-run orphanages. Most of these orphans had never known any type of physical affection, and some were severely disabled as a result.

These boys and girls were innocent victims of Romania's longtime dictator Nikolai Ceausescu. Under his regime, every able-bodied married woman was required to give birth to five children. These children were supposed to provide the workforce that would build Romania's future and turn the country into a global power.

Tragically, many families in that country were so poor that they couldn't provide for one or two children—much less five.

So the government built orphanages, where families were allowed to drop off children they were unable to care for. It's unthinkable that anyone would do that. But many of the women who left their children undoubtedly thought they were being merciful. Surely, the state would take better care of them than they were able to do.

The orphanages these children grew up in weren't cozy little cottages where children were bathed and fed, had fairy tales read to them, and then were lovingly tucked into cute little cribs in a brightly painted nursery. Think *Oliver Twist.* They were drab, often unheated warehouse-like structures where the children were left unattended in their beds for hours, and sometimes days, at a time. They had no toys to play with and they were rarely touched. Some never saw the light of day. They lived 24/7 in their cribs—like animals in a cage. The poor kids remained in these isolated, terrible conditions until they were eighteen years old, when they were dumped out into the world to fend for themselves.

The first people from outside Romania to set foot in those orphanages reported that many of the children did not react when they were talked to. Nor did they cry out or register surprise when they were exposed to sudden loud noises. Visitors told of seeing children rocking in their cribs as if in a catatonic state.

These kids weren't born with disabilities. They came into the world full of potential. But because they were deprived of the warm, loving touch of others, they wasted away in body, mind, and spirit.

> When the world found out about the plight of these children, many people got in line to adopt them.

Naturally, when the world found out about the plight of these children, many people got in line to adopt them. Two of our daughters, Gabriela and Katarina, came to us from Romania when they were both five years old. When Gabriela was an infant, her mother dropped her off at an orphanage in the town of Sebu, which is in the mountains of Romania. She spent five years there, and I must say that children in that small town had it a lot better than children in some other parts of Romania. The orphanage had a playground, and the kids did have some contact with children from the community. So her adjustment to her new life in America was fairly smooth. Gabi is now a beautiful young woman and the mother of our grandson, Anthony. She studied to become a hairdresser and works part-time in a salon owned by a friend of ours.

The transition was not so smooth for Kati. As an infant, Katarina was turned over to an orphanage in Bucharest, Romania's capital city. For five years, she never left her room. When we tried to bring her home, she screamed and struggled and didn't want to go. Everything frightened her. She couldn't get on the elevator. She screamed bloody murder when we tried to get her in our car, and threw a hysterical fit when she saw a dog on the street. It was heartbreaking to see her fear—and to realize how much she had missed out on during those first few years that should be so full of love and wonder. Kati is a beautiful young woman of twenty-four now. But the struggles she went through as an infant and young girl showed me that people just can't develop properly without the benefit of a gentle, loving touch.

> People just can't develop properly without the benefit of a gentle, loving touch.

Thousands of other children like Kati and Gabi were adopted into loving, caring families who loved them back to life and health.

But sadly, some were so broken that they never recovered. Many suffer from mental illness and will spend their lives in institutions. Others are homeless or struggle with addiction to drugs and alcohol. They are tragic examples of the severe damage that can be caused by the lack of a loving touch.[3]

> It seems that touch is the only one of the five basic senses that is deemed essential to human survival.

Over the last few years, scientists have coined the term *skin hunger* to explain the human need for physical contact. Research has shown that the skin, which is our largest organ, actually craves to be gently, lovingly touched. Doctors have found that premature babies actually do better when they are placed skin to skin on their mother's chest—or their father's chest.[4]

It seems that touch is the only one of the five basic senses that is deemed essential to human survival. People can survive without vision or hearing. The loss of one's ability to taste or smell is not fatal. But the lack of touch is deadly.

The Difference Between Men and Women

Every human being needs affection, but I believe this is especially true for women. It's how they're wired.

Ruth and I never tried to force our children into strict gender roles. We didn't insist that our boys play with toy cars, trucks, guns, and roll around in the dirt—but that's what they did. Nor did we tell our girls they had to be tender and nurturing, lovingly caring for their dolls and stuffed animals. And yet, for the most part, that's what they did.

> When it comes to giving our wives the physical affection they require, we are slow learners, stubborn, selfish, and spoiled.

Most of our girls loved to cuddle when they were little. They enjoyed sitting on Daddy's or Mommy's lap. The boys? Not so much. Yes, I know that some girls love to play rough and get dirty. And some boys have a strong affectionate and tender side. But I speak from a position of authority (remember, I'm a father of nineteen) when I say that girls are much more inclined to want to touch and be touched.

Don't be offended guys, but . . . may I speak frankly? The truth is that most of us suffer from what I call 4 S Disease. When it comes to giving our wives the physical affection they require, we are slow learners, stubborn, selfish, and spoiled.

Slow Learners

A husband wonders why his wife is acting distant or moody, asking her over and over again what's wrong and never realizing he could remedy the situation simply by putting his arms around her. Some men don't show their wives any physical affection . . . and then wonder why there's no passion in the bedroom. As Willard Harley says, "A man should work as carefully and patiently at showing affection in his marriage as he did when he and his wife dated."[5]

Stubborn

"Well, she's acting silly. If she wants a hug, let her come get one."

Your wife wants to know that you love her enough that you want to initiate affectionate contact. It doesn't count if she feels she had to "force" you into putting your arms around her for a while. She didn't have to force you when you were dating—why now?

Selfish

A man may get upset if his wife isn't ready and anxious to have sex whenever he feels like it. Yet he doesn't take the time to give his wife the nonsexual physical affection she needs. Nonsexual touching throughout the day sets the stage for intimacy later. Some men are more affectionate toward their dogs than toward their wives. But think, men, why does that dog rub against you, lick you, and cuddle up next to you? Because you pet him and play with him and laugh with him. Try the same with your wife.

Spoiled

We've been having it our way for a very long time. Let's turn the spoiling the other way around. If what I just said doesn't apply to you, then just keep on doing what you're already doing. But whatever you do, don't get angry and refuse to listen. I'm just trying to help you have the BEST marriage possible.

Women Need Affection

Studies show that most women who get involved in extramarital affairs do so because they are not getting the physical affection they need from their husbands. One of the best things you can do to affair-proof your marriage is to give your wife plenty of hugs, kisses, and other tenderness.

RUTH SAYS

Ladies, if you want the soft touches, the gentle kisses, and the hand-holding, make sure you look good enough to touch and kiss.

I can vividly remember my mother getting all dressed up and smelling really good on Friday afternoons before Daddy returned home from being out of town. Not that she looked bad the rest of the week, but Friday was special. As a result, she got the whistles and the hugs and the compliments, which put smiles on both of their faces—and the faces of my brother and me. My parents were never afraid or shy about kissing and hugging in front of us. It was natural. Perhaps that's why I'm so affectionate. I learned it from the best. I only hope my children learned it from Pat and me and carry on the tradition.

Here's the rule: If you want to be touched, be "touchworthy."

I will forever be thankful to Ruth's mother for the influence she had on Ruth in the area of being pleasing to the sight. Many times on Saturday mornings, we'll go out for breakfast at one of our favorite diners. I'm a people-watcher, and I've watched as other women come into the restaurant looking like they just woke up. Not Ruth.

If I suggest breakfast out, she says, "OK, I'd love to. Just give me fifteen minutes." Boy, is that fifteen minutes ever worth it! She goes to breakfast looking like a magazine layout. And it didn't take that long to get ready and look like the Queen of Sheba. Whenever Ruth leaves the house, she is totally done. And I appreciate that. I look at other women and I look at her, and I just smile, thinking, *Am I lucky or what?*

> Every woman is lovely in her own way and should do her best to let her God-given grace and beauty shine through.

Ladies, every man in the universe wants a "babe" on his arm, whether it's the first year of marriage or the sixtieth. And I don't mean that in a derogatory or condescending way at all. I just mean that men appreciate a woman taking the time to look her best—no matter what you're doing or where you're going. Ruth is always the most beautiful woman at a Little League game or at the Orlando Magic Gala Ball. Even if she's working from home, she takes the time to make herself look as good as possible. Ruth even looks good when she's working out in the weight room. Of course, I admit I am prejudiced because I know her beauty goes all the way through too. I believe that every woman is lovely in her own way and should do her best to let her God-given grace and beauty shine through. And the men should respond.

Willard Harley says, "Women need affection regularly and often, at least several times a day. A hug in the morning before getting out of bed, a kiss good-bye as he leaves for work, a call during the day, a card now and again in the mail, a big hug and kiss upon arriving home, seating her at the dinner table, holding hands in front of the television set—all these create the environment of affection."[6]

In *His Needs, Her Needs,* Dr. Harley has some terrific advice for men:

> To most women affection symbolizes security, protection, comfort, and approval, vitally important commodities in their eyes. When a husband shows his wife affection, he sends the following messages:
>
> 1. I'll take care of you and protect you. You are important to me, and I don't want anything to happen to you.
> 2. I'm concerned about the problems you face, and I am with you.
> 3. I think you've done a good job, and I'm so proud of you.
>
> A hug can say any and all of the above. Men need to understand how strongly women need these affirmations. *For the typical wife, there can hardly be enough of them.*[7]

Ruth is tough, yet gentle. She's hardworking, yet fun loving. She's strong, yet tender. She's independent, yet a terrific partner. She is the only woman I've ever known who has it all together. She remains calm in a crisis, yet cries while watching a movie on Lifetime or watching a grandchild take a first step. As we were writing this book, Ruth, like thousands of Americans across the country, received news that her company was cutting back on full-time presenters.

In the middle of the best speaking months she's had in a year, Ruth got the call from the HR department that she was one of the unlucky ones to be reduced to a contract consultant. That meant she lost any medical benefits and 401K contributions from the company. That part wasn't so bad, as she was already covered by my health care. But it also meant a reduction in days booked. That was hard for her.

One thing that makes Ruth such an incredible speaker is her belief in her material. She lives it—and loves it. She tells everyone, even outside her seminars, about how life-changing the content is. And it shows in her presentation. Being cut would be hard for anyone, but when it's a part of you, it can be devastating. She called me to tell me the bad news.

I immediately began to tell her what to do next and that everything would be OK. She listened quietly; I could hear the tears falling across the telephone line. I said, "I love you," told her good-bye, and hung up.

When the strongest woman I know is reduced to tears, it's time to take action. I left work and drove home.

I entered her office and found her just sitting, staring out the window. I didn't say a word. I walked over, lifted her to her feet, put my arms around her, and just held her and rocked her back and forth. She held on tight as I felt a few tears hit my shirt. After a while, she looked up and said, "Thank you. I needed that."

> When the strongest woman I know is reduced to tears, it's time to take action. I left work and drove home.

We didn't even talk about the situation; I just held her. She later told me that was the very best thing I could have done. By doing that, I made her feel treasured and comforted. She knew she could take the next step because she knew I would be there for her.

When I read the *The Language of Love,* I learned that more than 80 percent of a woman's desire for meaningful touch is not related to sex. A husband can show affection for his wife by doing simple things such as holding her hand, giving an unrequested back rub, or gently stroking her hair. Authors Gary Smalley and John Trent say that such gentle touching on a regular basis increases the wife's feelings of security. And that sets the stage for better communication, emotional bonding, and romance.[8]

If you're not used to being affectionate, it may take you some time to learn this new "habit." At first, it may seem awkward and forced, as if it isn't real. But don't give up. Keep on trying, and if your wife says, "Oh, you're just putting on an act," say, "No, I'm trying to show you how much I love you."

Tell her, "I want to be better at giving you what you need. I just need you to help me become the husband you want me to be."

It takes guts to be this open and honest about your own shortcomings. And if there's anything a wife wants as much as love and affection, it's a husband who's willing to be open and honest.

Men Need Affection Too

It's no secret that most men have high-performance engines when it comes to our sex drive. We're like the sports car that can go from zero to sixty in four seconds flat. This is why our wives tend to be suspicious when we start showing affection that isn't designed to steer them toward the bedroom.

And yet, we are missing something that is vital to our emotional and physical health if we are not enjoying regular nonsexual affection from the lady in our lives. Now perhaps I should define what I mean by nonsexual. My feeling is that any skin-on-skin contact between a husband and wife is going to be sexual to a certain degree. Holding hands is sexual. A hug is sexual. Certainly, kissing is sexual. But it doesn't have to go any further than this. We husbands need to understand that hugging and kissing don't always have to lead to sex. And we shouldn't pout and act like spoiled brats at those times.

> Did you know that briefly hugging your wife and holding her hand for ten minutes can protect your heart by reducing the harmful effects of stress?

Did you know that briefly hugging your wife and holding her hand for ten minutes can protect your heart by reducing the harmful effects of stress? It's true.

According to an article in *USA Today*, psychologist Karen Grewen of the University of North Carolina–Chapel Hill says that such affectionate contact before a tough day can "carry over and protect you throughout the day." Grewen conducted a study in which one hundred adults were told to hold hands with their spouses while watching a pleasant, ten-minute video. Afterward, the couples were told to hug for twenty seconds.

At the same time, another group of eighty-five adults rested quietly without contact with their spouses.

Then everyone in both groups was urged to start talking about a recent event that made them feel angry or stressed. After that, all participants had their blood pressure and pulse checked. According to the article, "Blood pressure soared in the no-contact people. Their systolic (upper) reading jumped 24 points, more than double the rise for huggers, and their diastolic (lower) also rose significantly higher." Furthermore, "Heart rate increased 10 beats a minute for those without contact compared with five beats a minute for huggers."[9]

Affection Checklist

Remember Andy, the gentleman Ruth wrote about who scheduled things like "Did you tell Joann 'I love you' today?" into his BlackBerry? Perhaps when you read about him you thought, *But shouldn't affection come naturally? Should I really have to schedule it?* Well, of course it should come naturally. But it is easy to let it fall by the wayside, especially if you and your spouse are running through stressful days packed full of activity.

Affection should not be a duty. It should not be mechanical. No one should say, "OK, I told my wife I love her. Now I can scratch that off my to-do list." I am not offering the following as a list that should go into your Franklin Planner, but rather as a guideline to help you ensure that you and your spouse are giving each other the affection you need:

- Start every day with a hug and kiss.
- Tell each other "I love you" before you go your separate ways for the day.
- Call each other at least once during the day to see how things are going.
- Send each other love notes or cards every once in a while. If you are both online for much of the day, surprise your spouse with an e-card just to say "I love you."
- Thoughtfully remember special days such as anniversaries, birthdays, and other important occasions. (For example, if your wife lost her father a few years ago, and the date of his death always makes her sad, show her you care by giving her some special attention on that day. It will mean more to her than you can imagine.)
- Set aside some alone time for each other every evening to talk about what went on during the day and what lies ahead tomorrow (and the rest of the week).

- Find time to pray together before bedtime.
- Give each other a hug and kiss and say "I love you" before you go to bed.
- Make it a regular practice to go to bed at the same time.
- Snuggle often.

That covers affectionate touching. *Now* we're going to talk about sex.

Reflect  & Discuss

1. Read Mark 10:13-16. What does this passage say to you about God's affection for you as his child?

2. If Christians are "the hands and feet of Jesus," what are some specific ways you can be a channel of God's blessing to your husband or wife?

3. Read Matthew 14:34-36. What does this passage say to you about Jesus' willingness to touch and be touched?

4. How would you rate yourself when it comes to showing physical (nonsexual) affection to your spouse?

_____ Great
_____ Good
_____ Not so good
_____ I'd rather not say

5. How does your spouse rate you in this area? (The only way you can find out is to ask!)

_____ Great
_____ Good
_____ Not so good
_____ I'd rather not say

6. How would you rate your spouse when it comes to giving you the affection you need?

_____ Great
_____ Good
_____ Not so good
_____ I'd rather not say

7. To what degree, if any, do you feel that lack of physical affection has been a problem in your marriage?

8. In what ways do you need to do a better job of showing physical affection? How can you do this? And will you commit to set aside some time to talk openly with your spouse about the affection *you* need?

9. For the next week, take at least five minutes every night to sit on the couch and hold each other. (Take our word for it. You'll both love it.)

Chapter 11

God Created Sex . . . and It Was Good

THERE'S NOTHING BETTER THAN GOOD SEX. BUT BAD SEX? A PEANUT BUTTER AND JELLY SANDWICH IS BETTER THAN BAD SEX.

—BILLY JOEL

The last ingredient I want to discuss that goes into the BEST marriage possible is the sexual love that God created. Everything he created is naturally good, no matter how much Satan tries to corrupt it. And boy, does he try!

The late singer Larry Norman, the father of Christian rock, once wrote a song called "Why Should the Devil Have All the Good Music?"

Good question. Here's another one: "Why should the devil have all the sex?" After all, as we just said, God invented it.

The truth is, the devil *doesn't* have all the sex. He does have the market cornered on perverted, cheap, casual, meaningless, destructive sex. But when it comes to good sex, it's all about God and his ordinance of marriage—a committed, lifetime relationship between one man and one woman.

I believe that Satan's perversion of sex is one of his greatest victories on his war against humankind. There are so many parallels in the natural world—good things that are dangerous and destructive when used the wrong way. For instance, there's almost nothing on earth that can compete with the comfort of a crackling fire in a fireplace on a cold night. But if that fire should get out of control, it could burn the whole house down. Similarly, water is necessary for human life. But if your body takes in too much water, you will drown. Used properly, nuclear power can provide energy for an entire city. Yet a nuclear explosion could destroy that same city, kill thousands of people, and leave dangerous levels of radiation in the soil.

> Used properly, nuclear power can provide energy for an entire city. Yet a nuclear explosion could destroy that same city, kill thousands of people, and leave dangerous levels of radiation in the soil.

Improper sex causes tremendous misery. We've seen it in the AIDS pandemic that has killed twenty-five million people worldwide and created more than eleven million orphans in Africa.[1] We've seen it in the trafficking of innocent women and girls—as many as two million of them forced against their will to serve as "sex workers."[2] And of course, we've seen it in the thousands of American families broken up because of adultery.

The Bible teaches us that, when used properly, sex is very good. Genesis 1:31 says, "God looked over all he had made, and he saw that it was *very* good!" (emphasis added). This came right after God invented sex. Just a few verses earlier, he created man and woman and told them to "be fruitful and multiply" (vv. 27, 28).

There is only one way we can do this, and that is by having sexual relations. God could have designed us so that we reproduced asexually, splitting to form another person when the time was right, like the amoeba do (or is it the paramecium? I never could get them straight). But I'm glad he didn't.

Ruth and I are not sex therapists, and this book is not a sex manual. There are already dozens of excellent books on sex written from a Judeo-Christian perspective. Nevertheless, we both feel that it would be irresponsible to just breeze by the subject as if sex doesn't exist. Talk about ignoring the elephant in the room!

An Expression of Love

The first thing we want to say about sex is that God intends for it to be an expression of married love between one man and one woman who are committed to each other for life.

Have you ever wondered why the world's population is so closely divided between males and females? Of the millions of babies born every year, about half are girls and half are boys. It's not exactly 50-50, but it's pretty close. I believe this is another validation of God's plan for marriage: one man and one woman together for life.

> The first thing we want to say about sex is that God intends for it to be an expression of married love between one man and one woman who are committed to each other for life.

RUTH SAYS

I remember reading an article several years ago about the dilemma young Chinese men are facing. Apparently, there is a real shortage of young women in China. The Chinese government, as you probably know, allows couples to produce only one child, due to the overpopulation of the country. Couples who produce boys are rewarded and looked upon with favor in society. Couples who produce girls are shunned.

As a result, according to the reporter, couples often gave the baby girls to orphanages so they could try again for a boy. In many cases, these little girls were then adopted out to parents all over the world. Couples who chose to keep their girls hoped their daughters would eventually show athletic prowess and be taken by the government to train for gymnastics or some other sport. In these cases, where the girls became good athletes, the parents were shown favor; however, the parents lost the child to the state.

Tragically, it seems that some couples decided to kill their daughters at birth. This is just too horrible for me to imagine. But because of this government edict, there are now fewer young women in China than young men. They have fooled with God's

50-50 plan, and the young men have no one to date and eventually marry. It is causing deep depression among young Chinese men.

Some are relying on houses of prostitution to fill the void, but of course, this leads to more acute depression and even guilt. Some, on the other hand, are leaving China (and their families) to find true love somewhere else in the world.[3] How tragic to have to leave your homeland simply to find love. But they are doing it for one reason: God did not mean for man to live alone.

Every man needs love, and he needs it from one woman who is committed to him. How simple it would be to eliminate the disease of depression among young men in China—if only their government would follow God's plan. It would also eliminate the guilt of promiscuity.

God clearly hates sexual promiscuity of any kind and desires that sex take place only within the context of marriage. Here are some words of God that bear that out:

- "You can't say that our bodies were made for sexual immorality. They were made for the Lord, and the Lord cares about our bodies" (1 Corinthians 6:13).
- "Run from sexual sin! No other sin so clearly affects the body as this one does. For sexual immorality is a sin against your own body" (1 Corinthians 6:18).
- "Let there be no sexual immorality, impurity, or greed among you. Such sins have no place among God's people" (Ephesians 5:3).
- "God's will is for you to be holy, so stay away from all sexual sin" (1 Thessalonians 4:3).
- "The husband should fulfill his wife's sexual needs, and the wife should fulfill her husband's needs. The wife gives authority over her body to her

husband, and the husband gives authority over his body to his wife. Do not deprive each other of sexual relations, unless you both agree to refrain from sexual intimacy for a limited time so you can give yourselves more completely to prayer. Afterward, you should come together again so that Satan won't be able to tempt you because of your lack of self-control" (1 Corinthians 7:3-5).

It's so important to keep the home fires burning. If a married couple does not enjoy a healthy sex life, Satan will tempt them in this area. How many Christian leaders have been brought down by sexual scandal? How many political careers have been ruined? How many families have been torn apart? Thousands? Hundreds of thousands? Maybe even millions.

Look at what happened to David, the greatest king in the history of Israel. This is a man who took on the mighty giant Goliath in a one-on-one death match. The Bible refers to David as "a man after [God's] own heart" (1 Samuel 13:14). And yet his sexual sin tore his family apart and very nearly ripped the kingdom out of his hands.

> "The husband should fulfill his wife's sexual needs, and the wife should fulfill her husband's needs."

Perhaps you remember the story from 2 Samuel 11, 12. David was walking around the roof of the palace one night when he saw a woman named Bathsheba bathing nearby. She was beautiful, and he began to burn with lust. He wanted her, and as king, he felt he was entitled to have her. The Bible doesn't tell us whether Bathsheba was trying to get David's attention. Perhaps she was an innocent victim who was afraid to refuse the king's advances. But whatever the case, when he sent for her, she came and slept with him.

Not long after that, she sent word that she was pregnant.

Now David was in trouble. Bathsheba's husband, Uriah, was off fighting for his country. He hadn't been home in weeks. He would know the child wasn't his, and according to the law of Moses, the penalty for adultery was execution!

What could David do?

David sent word to the battlefield that Uriah should be sent back to Jerusalem, ostensibly to report on how the war was going. Uriah came to the palace but refused to go home to be with his wife. He felt it wouldn't be right to enjoy the comfort of his own bed while his comrades-in-arms were sleeping on the battlefield. David tried to get Uriah drunk, but he still refused to go home.

That's when David compounded one terrible sin with another. He sent Uriah back to the front, instructing his commander to put him in the fiercest part of the battle so he would be killed. That is exactly what happened.

> When sexual lust is allowed to burn wild, it can be worse than a southern California wildfire, devouring everything in its path.

When God sent a prophet to David to confront him about what he had done, David completely and sincerely repented. Because of this, God did not demand his life nor take the kingdom away from him. But David was never again completely at peace. The child that was born to Bathsheba died. Another son, Absalom, launched a rebellion against him. Read through the psalms, and you can see how David's sin often bore down on him and seemed to separate him from God.

When sexual lust is allowed to burn wild, it can be worse than a southern California wildfire, devouring everything in its path.

Cheating Brings Tragedy

I read an interesting story about a family of bald eagles.[4] As a webcam captured the drama, the Internet made it possible for many people to watch what was, in effect, the breakup of a family.

"After raising several offspring in previous seasons, the mother again laid new eggs in the spring. But then a young female invaded their happy home. When Dad started cavorting around with her, Mom disappeared and the life in the abandoned eggs died."

Everyone who had come to love the eagles was distraught and wanted the original couple to get back together. Biologists had explained that you can't expect birds to have human values, but the eagle fans couldn't suppress their sadness.

The writer "wondered if they knew that God feels much the same way about human family breakups." In Malachi 2:10-16, we see God's view of marriage that symbolizes his covenant with his people, and we see how strongly he feels about wanting marriages to last.

This little illustration about a family of eagles reminds us of the destruction that can come upon human families through marital infidelity. Do yourself a favor. Run from temptation.

Understand Your Man

Ladies, this is important, so please read carefully: A man's need for sex is every bit as strong as a woman's need for affection. Maybe stronger. There is nothing wrong with your marriage just because your husband wants sex way more often than you do. That's almost always the case in any marriage. So try not to get too upset if he comes on strong. He may even realize that he's behaving improperly, but he just can't help it. Don't think your husband loves you only for your body. That's not true. He loves you for who you are—your heart, soul, and mind—but he loves your body too.

I get a kick out of reading about God's creation of Eve in the second chapter of Genesis. The Bible doesn't quite put it this way, but I get the sense that when Adam saw Eve for the first time, his eyes bugged out and he said, "Hot dog! Wrap her up, God, I'll take her!" Or something like that.

Most men are easily aroused. A guy may start out just wanting to give his wife some affection, but before he knows what's happened, he's trying to steer her into the bedroom. His wife has a kink in her back and asks him if he'll give her a quick back rub. She appreciates his willingness to do it, but gets irritated that he can't seem to do it without getting excited.

Many marriages get into trouble because of arguments about sex. She thinks he wants too much sex. He thinks she's a cold fish. And often, the more he pushes her for sex, the colder she gets. I can't give you a simple solution that's going to change all this. But I know that the answer to every problem in marriage begins with understanding and communication—so talk about it. Tell each other what you need. Be open!

Understand Your Woman (Well, Try!)

Guys, you need to understand that your wife has a different view of sex than you do. A woman wants to be held. She enjoys the closeness of sex, the physical intimacy with her husband. For a man, making love can be a purely physical act. For a woman, this is rarely the case. For her, making love to her life partner is something sacred—a union of two souls. In general, she comes closer than her husband to understanding sexual love the way God intended it to be. Guys, it's about a lot more than sex.

- You can't ignore your wife all evening and expect her to want to make love to you as soon as the lights are out.
- You can't talk to her in a belittling or condescending tone and expect that she's going to warm up to you in bed.
- You can't get up from the dinner table, go plop yourself down in front of the television, and leave her to clean up, without expecting it to affect her mood later in the evening.
- You can't walk around like a slob, not taking care of your personal hygiene—like brushing your teeth and clipping your nails—and expect her to be burning with desire for you. It's just not going to happen.

> We can demand sex because it's our right and leave our wives feeling cold and empty inside. Or we can treat our wives in such a way that they want to love us.

I hope it doesn't sound like I'm picking on you. You probably don't do any of these things, but it's easy to fall into bad habits without even realizing it. I understand that, as we saw in 1 Corinthians, a husband has a right to his wife's body. But we have a choice. We can demand sex because it's our right and leave our wives feeling cold and empty inside. Or we can treat our wives in such a way that they want to love us. I don't have to tell you which of these will make for a happier spouse.

Talk to Each Other About Sex

Married couples talk to each other about all sorts of things: finances, disciplining the children, plans for the future, and where they're going to go for vacation this year. But sadly, most don't talk to each other about sex. Why not? Because they're too embarrassed? Because it's not something polite people talk about (even if they are married to each other)?

Sex is too important to ignore. How often would you like to make love? When? Would you like a bit more hugging and cuddling? Do you wish your partner would stop eating food loaded with onions and garlic? Talk to each other about it!

How can you bring up such a difficult subject? Start by telling your spouse what you *do* like about the way he or she loves you. Don't criticize or nag. That is definitely not going to help. Remind your spouse of your love and that you want every part of your life together to be good, including your sex life. Then *gently* explain what you'd like to see changed.

And please give your spouse a chance to give his or her input. Two sensible, mature adults should be able to have a discussion about their love life without starting World War III.

Give Your Wife Some Help

Want to do something that will really get your wife's motor running?

Try doing the dishes. Or cleaning up after dinner. Or better yet, *cooking* dinner. Or do what I do—take her out!

Many women are simply too exhausted for lovemaking. Your wife may think about it during the day. She may look forward to a rendezvous with you later on. But by the time the opportunity comes, she's just too tired.

> You've probably heard it said that "a man may work from sunup to sundown, but a woman's work is never done." Let's retire that old proverb.

If you suspect that this might be the case in your marriage, ask yourself what you can do to take some of the load off your wife's shoulders. Perhaps you could afford to hire a cleaning service to come in once a week or a couple of times a month. Or maybe you could pitch in a bit more with the kids so she can have more time for herself.

You've probably heard it said that "a man may work from sunup to sundown, but a woman's work is never done." Let's retire that old proverb. A well-rested wife is a happier wife. And a happier wife makes for a happier husband.

And while you're at it, maybe you should get some help for yourself.

Does this sound familiar? A couple crawls in bed at the end of the day and turns out the light. "How are you feeling tonight?" he asks.

"I'm OK," she replies. "Just kind of tired. How about you?"

"I'm tired too."

"Well, why were you asking? Did you want to . . . you know . . ."

He sighs, "Well, I was thinking about it. But to tell you the truth, I *am* pretty tired."

"Me too," she says, patting his leg. "Maybe we'll feel more like it tomorrow night."

"Yeah, maybe so."

Many people of both sexes are just too exhausted to make love.

If you saw yourself in that scenario, then you and your wife both need to figure out how you can simplify your life and have more time for just relaxing and enjoying each other's company.

Learn to Enjoy Sex

There are two solutions to every problem:

- You can change the problem.
- You can change your attitude about the problem.

Unfortunately, many married women have developed a bad attitude about sex. If you're one of them, then it's time to start working on changing your attitude. It *can* be done.

Willard Harley says that "many women don't understand their own sexuality well enough to know how to enjoy meeting a husband's compelling need for sex. In order to satisfy her husband sexually a wife must also feel satisfied. I try to encourage wives not to simply make their bodies available on a more regular basis; rather they should commit themselves to learning to enjoy the sex relationship as much as their husbands do."[5]

I know there are plenty of reasons why some women don't like sex. One of these has to do with the fact that they've always considered sex to be "nasty." This may be especially true of girls who were brought up in overly strict homes, where sexuality was not treated as a normal, natural part of life. One woman in her fifties told me about the punishment she got when she was three years old and her mom caught her "playing doctor" with the little boy about the same age who lived next door.

The spanking she got would have been forgotten years ago if her well-meaning mother had not combined it with some harsh words about what a horrible, nasty thing she had done. No wonder she felt inhibited and embarrassed about the marriage bed later on in life.

RUTH SAYS

I'm one of the lucky ones. My mother was no-nonsense when it came to talking to my brother and me about anything, and that included sex. Here's what she taught us about sex. (And it's quite different from the example above.)

She told us sex was the most beautiful and enjoyable thing a man and woman could experience—*IF* (big if) they were married. It was not recreation; it was a blessing, but only within the boundary of marriage. My mother was not a prude, even though she was a die-hard Christian. She believed every word of the Bible, and the Bible clearly tells us that sex between a husband and wife is a wonderful thing. Just read a chapter or two in the Song of Solomon. And as you do, keep in mind that this was inspired by God, written for our edification and education. It's romantic and almost erotic, but that's what God intended for a man and woman in marriage.

> The Bible clearly tells us that sex between a husband and wife is a wonderful thing. Just read a chapter or two in the Song of Solomon.

I get so angry sometimes when I see how sex is dirtied up in our movies and magazines. I believe the reason so many celebrities have relationship problems is because they are not doing what God intended. If they were, they'd be much happier. And they're obviously not happy, as evidenced by all the breakups, drug abuse, and other scandalous behavior.

Sex is only nasty when abused; sex is beautiful and wonderful when done the way God made it. That is the message I've passed on to my girls, and I hope that will be the message you pass on to your children. How can they possibly enjoy that part of marriage if they've been taught that it's dirty or nasty? Please, please—don't do that to your children, or they'll end up like the fifty-year-old woman mentioned above.

Another reason why women don't like sex is because, frankly, their husbands aren't good at it. They don't try to please their wives, but just take what they want. If this is the case with you, sit your husband down and tell him what you really want and need from him. If that doesn't do any good, ask him to go with you to see a therapist.

Finally, many women don't like sex because they have low self-esteem. They compare themselves with the glamorous models they see on TV or in the movies, and they feel they can't measure up. "I just don't like my body," they say.

If you feel this way about yourself, you're not alone. Remember the quotes from Elizabeth Taylor, Gwyneth Paltrow, Michelle Pfeiffer, and the other beauties I mentioned in chapter 4? I could have gone on with similar quotes for ten pages or more! Recently, I came across this one from *American Idol* winner Kelly Clarkson, who sat down to an interview with Elysa Gardner of *USA Today*: "Do you know what it's like when you've just woken up, and your lips are all huge and your face is swollen? Every time I talk, I keep licking my lips. They must look monstrous. I must look like a platypus."[6]

Cute Kelly Clarkson looking like a platypus? Hardly. You may not like the way you look, but your husband certainly does. Try to find some gratification in that. If you weren't beautiful in his eyes, he wouldn't want to make love to you. Learn to see yourself as the beautiful creature God sees when he looks at you. Healthy self-esteem can be a great aphrodisiac.

Enjoy the Afterglow

Another thing many women complain about regarding sex is that when a man is done making love, he's done.

"He just loses interest," one woman said. "He rolls over, goes to sleep, and is snoring in five minutes."

Not good, fella.

Your wife wants you to hold her and be tender with her—and not make her feel as if the only thing you're really interested in is your own satisfaction. Strangely enough, it's when you are satisfied that her need for intimacy is at its peak.

It's important to stay close to her for a while. Cuddle. Tell her you love her and how much you enjoy having her next to you. I believe this will bring on a noticeable increase in her sexual thermostat. And that can't be bad!

So there you have it. *T* stands for *touch* in our BEST game plan. Affectionate touching is absolutely vital to your marriage. And God invented sex. Good sex. Good things happen when we follow his plan for this and every other area of our lives.

Reflect & Discuss

1. Has anything you read in this chapter altered your attitude about sex? If so, describe how your attitude has changed.

2. If sex is a gift from God, what can you do to encourage a proper, godly understanding of sex?

3. Look back at the Bible verses concerning sex that were referenced in this chapter. If the Scriptures are clear regarding God's thoughts about premarital sex and his desire that sex be reserved only for married partners, why do you think there is such rampant sexual promiscuity today?

4. What are the three most important things you've learned from this book?

5. List at least four ways you will change your behavior as a result of what you've read.

6. What does your spouse say is the most important thing he or she has learned from this book?

7. What are some of the things your spouse will do differently after reading this book?

Not the End, but a Beginning

So what's the bottom line when it comes to marriage? We want to close by sharing a story that is special to us.

I've developed a rather grueling hobby in my old age: I run marathons. Actually, some wouldn't call it running. It is more like a diligent and upbeat walk. But realizing that misery thrives on company, and being the heady salesman that I am, early in our marriage I convinced Ruth to run them with me.

So in 1997, just ten days after our wedding, we ran the Boston Marathon together. At the 9-mile mark, Ruth pulled up, told me her knee was hurt, and that she had to stop at a first-aid station. Her parting words were: "Keep going. Don't quit. I love you."

I pushed onward. For eleven miles, I moved along by myself with thoughts of Ruth bandying about in my weary head. *How disappointed she must be! I hope she doesn't feel that she let me down. I hope she doesn't feel that I've deserted her.* It was at the 20-mile mark that I wheezed up Boston's Heartbreak Hill, my body fading, my legs cramping, and my heart fluttering. I thought I was about to hit the proverbial wall.

And then I heard a voice from behind me. "Paaatrick!" Was someone calling my name?

I heard it again, only louder this time. "Paaaatrick!" I peered over my right shoulder and thought I was hallucinating. But I wasn't. There she was, running toward me in her canary yellow shirt. She was waving at me with a huge smile on her face. She'd had her knee treated and had run eleven miles by herself to catch up to me. We ran the last six miles together.

At the last mile marker—mile 26—Ruth stopped for a moment to put on her lipstick before we turned the final corner. (You know how they say "It ain't over till the fat lady sings." Well, for Ruth, it ain't over till the lipstick goes on.) As we turned onto Boylston Street, we held hands and ran that last quarter mile to the finish line.

There are two didactic branches to this story. The first is that I might be the slowest marathon runner in the history of the Boston Marathon. But we'll concern ourselves with that at another time.

> Marathons are a reflection of life—and marriage. You get to practice "not quitting" for about five hours.

The second, of course, is that perseverance is paramount—that nothing is accomplished by stopping altogether, by melting beneath circumstances. Ruth did not give up on finding me or finishing the marathon with me.

This story is the most literal example I can evoke of man's ability to push ahead amid seemingly insurmountable obstacles. Marathons are a reflection of life—and marriage. You get to practice "not quitting" for about five hours.

I learned right then that Ruth won't quit when life gets hard or she has setbacks and heartaches. Through twelve years of marriage and through raising children, Ruth is tenacious just like she was at the Boston Marathon in her canary yellow shirt.

Keep running toward the goal—together. If your partner falls behind, wait for him. If she's exhausted, encourage her to keep going. Together you can reach your dreams.

You *can* have the BEST, happy, fulfilling marriage, and that's the way God always intended it to be!

Acknowledgments

With deep appreciation we acknowledge the support and guidance of the following people who helped make this book possible:

Special thanks to Alex Martins, Bob Vander Weide, and Rich DeVos of the Orlando Magic.

Thanks to my writing partner, Dave Wimbish, for his superb contributions in shaping this manuscript.

Hats off to four dependable associates—my assistant Latria Leak, my trusted and valuable colleague Andrew Herdliska, my creative consultant Ken Hussar, and my ace typist Fran Thomas.

Hearty thanks also go to our friends at Standard Publishing. Thank you all for believing that we had something important to share and for providing the support and the forum to say it. Sincere thanks to Dale Reeves for your continued support and encouragement.

And finally, gratitude and appreciation go to our wonderful and supportive children and grandchildren. They are truly the backbone of our lives.

—Pat and Ruth Williams

Chapter 1

Epigraph. Martin Luther, www.brainyquote.com.

Chapter 2

1. "Divorce Statistics Collection: Summary of Findings So Far," Americans for Divorce Reform, www.divorcereform.org (accessed March 18, 2009).

2. Information in this section was taken from "U.S. Divorce Rates for Various Faith Groups, Age Groups & Geographic Areas," Ontario Consultants on Religious Tolerance, www.religioustolerance.org (accessed January 11, 2009).

3. Ed Wheat, *Love Life for Every Married Couple* (Grand Rapids, MI: Zondervan Publishing House, 1981), 27–28.

4. William Penn, www.brainyquote.com.

5. Tim A. Gardner, "Marital Drift," www.ChristianityToday.com, summer 1999 (accessed March 15, 2009).

6. Information in this section was taken from Linda J. Waite and others, "Does Divorce Make People Happy?: Findings from a Study of Unhappy Marriages," Institute for American Values, www.americanvalues.org, 2002 (accessed March 19, 2009).

7. Simon Presland, "How to Fight Fair in a Marriage," www.lifetoolsfor women.com (accessed March 15, 2009).

8. https://www.stephencovey.com/7habits/7habits.php (accessed July 8, 2009).

9. Ogden Nash, www.thinkexist.com.

Chapter 3

Epigraph. Barbara de Angelis, www.brainyquote.com.

1. "The Night the Roof Fell In," *The Dick Van Dyke Show*, written by Carl Reiner and John Whedon, originally broadcast November 21, 1962, http://www.archive.org (accessed June 18, 2009).

2. www.stephencovey.com.

3. Stephen R. Covey, *The 7 Habits of Highly Effective People* (New York: Free Press, 1989), 79–80.

4. Information in this section was taken from Shruti S. Poulsen, PhD, "A Fine Balance: The Magic Ratio to a Healthy Relationship," Purdue University's *Purdue Extension*, CFS-744-W, March 2008.

5. Squire Rushnell and Louise DuArt, *Couples Who Pray: The Most Intimate Act Between a Man and a Woman*, book synopsis, http://search.barnesandnoble.com/Couples-Who-Pray/Squire-Rushnell/e/9780785227946 (accessed July 9, 2009).

6. Richard Exley, *The Making of a Man: Devotions for the Challenges That Men Face in Family and Career* (Tulsa: Honor Books, 1993), chapter 18.

7. Dennis Rainey, "Prayer: The Secret to a Lasting Marriage," www.familylife.com (accessed March 18, 2009).

8. www.stephencovey.com.

Chapter 4

1. Sources for quotations in this section are: A—www.famousquotesandauthors.com; B, C, D—www.brainyquote.com; E—www.quotelucy.com.

2. Personal conversation with James Dobson.

3. Truett Cathy, www.mondaymemo.com (accessed June 18, 2009).

4. All statistics on pornography in this section are taken from "Statistics and Information on Pornography in the USA," www.blazinggrace.org (accessed February 7, 2009).

5. Cicero, http://books.google.com.

6. Gary Chapman, *The Five Love Languages: How to Express Heartfelt Commitment to Your Mate* (Chicago: Northfield Publishing, 1992, 1995), 15.

7. Ibid., 38.

8. Ibid., quoted from http://search.barnesandnoble.com/Five-Love-Languages/Gary-Chapman/e/9781881273158/#CHP.

9. "Statistics and Information on Pornography in the USA," www.blazinggrace.org (accessed February 7, 2009).

Chapter 5

Epigraph. Helen Keller, www.thinkexist.com.

1. John Wooden, *Wooden*, http://books.google.com.

2. Ernest Hemingway, www.brainyquote.com.

3. Zelda West-Meads, quoted in "The Horror of a Silent Holiday" by Wendy Holden, http://www.dailymail.co.uk/femail/article-129898/The-horror-silent-holiday.html (accessed June 18, 2009).

4. As told in *Parade* magazine, April 6, 2008, 7.

Chapter 6

Epigraph. John Steinbeck, www.famousquotesandauthors.com.

1. Euripides, www.famousquotesandauthors.com.

2. Matthew Henry, www.thinkexist.com.

Chapter 7

Epigraph. Paul Tillich, www.quotes.possumstew.com.

1. Nelson Mandela story, told by Philip Yancey in *Rumors of Another World*, sourced from Herbert Vander Lugt, "Redemptive Revenge," *Our Daily Bread*, October 28, 2005, www.rbc.org (accessed July 9, 2009).

2. Corrie ten Boom, "Corrie Ten Boom, Story on Forgiving," www.familylife education.org (accessed March 20, 2009). Originally published in *Guideposts* magazine, copyright 1972 by Guideposts Associates, Inc., Carmel, New York 10512.

3. Mark Atteberry, *So Much More Than Sexy* (Cincinnati, OH: Standard Publishing, 2009), 127.

4. Jamie Buckingham, *Risky Living* (Plainfield, NJ: Logos International, 1976), 91.

5. Brennan Manning, *The Ragamuffin Gospel* (Sisters, OR: Multnomah Publishers, 1990), 115–116.

6. Dr. Frederic Luskin in *Redbook* magazine; no other information available.

Chapter 8

Epigraph. William Arthur Ward, www.thinkexist.com.

1. Information in this section was taken from Bill Russell with Alan Steinberg, *Red and Me: My Coach, My Lifelong Friend* (New York: HarperCollins, 2009), 37.

2. Song title: "Woman You Wanna Be." Writer credits: Steven A. Dean/ Brian Gene White/ Karyn Williams. Copyright © Bridge Building Music, Inc./ Dino's Song Shop (BMI)/Multisongs, Inc./Songs From The White House/Universal Music—Brentwood Benson Tunes (SESAC). All rights for the world on behalf of Dino's Song Shop administered by Bridge Building Music (BMI). All rights for the world on behalf of Songs from the White House administered by Multisongs, Inc (SESAC). All right reserved. Used by permission. You can listen to this song at Karyn's Web site, www.karynwilliams.com.

3. Willard F. Harley Jr., "Why Women Leave Men," www.marriagebuilders. com (accessed March 19, 2009).

4. William F. Harley Jr., *His Needs, Her Needs* (Old Tappan, NJ: Fleming H. Revell, 1986), 58.

5. Ann Landers, quoted in "Wisdom and Humor," www.stfrancisofficepark. com (accessed March 17, 2009).

Chapter 9

1. "World's Longest-Married Couple Clock Up 80 Years," www.goodnews blog.com, posted May 31, 2005 (accessed March 17, 2009).

2. Garrison Keillor, "Suffering Brings Wisdom, but So Does Fun," www. jewishworldreview.com, October 6, 2005 (accessed March 17, 2009).

3. www.sermonillustrations.com.

4. "USC Player's Breakout Interviews," www.orangebowl.org (accessed March 17, 2009).

5. Bonnie Jenkins, "Health Benefits of Laughter: Send in the Clowns," www.healthier-you.com (accessed February 17, 2009).

6. Information in this section was taken from "Marvelous Bible Quotes," www.bibleresources.bible.com (accessed March 17, 2009).

Chapter 10

Epigraph. Tom Peters, www.tompeters.com.

1. "Need for Touch," www.thewellspring.com, 2009 (accessed March 18, 2009).

2. Amy Nappa, *A Woman's Touch: The Fingerprints Left Behind* (West Monroe, LA: Howard Books, 1991), quoted from www.heartlight.org (accessed July 17, 2009).

3. Information on this subject is readily available online. For example: "The Orphanages," http://www.csuchico.edu/engl/faculty and "Country Report: Romania," http://www.iabolish.org/slavery_today/country_reports/ro.html (both accessed June 19, 2009).

4. http://pettawaypursuitfoundation.org/preemiecare.html (accessed June 19, 2009).

5. Harley, *His Needs, Her Needs*, 37.

6. Ibid., 36.

7. Ibid., 29.

8. Gary Smalley and John Trent, *The Language of Love* (Carol Stream, IL: Tyndale House Publishers, 2006 edition), 185.

9. Karen Grewen, quoted by Marilyn Elias, "Study: Hugs Warm the Heart, and May Protect It," www.usatoday.com, posted March 10, 2003 (accessed March 18, 2009).

Chapter 11

Epigraph. Billy Joel, www.thinkexist.com.

1. http://www.avert.org/worldstats.html.

2. Paul Shepard, "Sex Trade Flourishing, US Says," http://www.friends-partners.org, February 23, 2000 (accessed June 1, 2009).

3. To read more about the situation in China, see "China Grapples with Legacy of Its 'Missing Girls,'" http://www.msnbc.com (accessed June 7, 2009).

4. Story from Julie Ackerman Link, "A Sad Split," *Our Daily Bread*, February 26, 2009.

5. Harley, *His Needs, Her Needs,* 51.

6. Elysa Gardner, "Former 'Idol' Kelly Clarkson Has All She Ever Wanted," www.usatoday.com, March 8, 2009.